בס"ד

זיו השמות
What's in a Name?

Laws and customs
regarding the naming of children
and related topics

by
Rabbi Y. Z. Wilhelm

Translated by
Rabbi Shimon Neubort

5758 • 1998

זיו השמות
Ziv HaShemos
Copyright © 1988
by
Rabbi Y.Z. Wilhelm

•

English Translation
"What's in a Name?"
Copyright © 1998

Published and Distributed by

S. I. E. Publications
788 Eastern Parkway
Brooklyn N.Y. 11213
(718) 778-5436

Rabbi Y. Z. Wilhelm
25 Balfour Place
Brooklyn, N.Y. 11225
(718) 604-3473

All rights reserved. No part of this publication may be reproduced in any form or by any means, including photocopying and translation, without permission in writing from the copyright holder or the publisher.

ISBN 1-8814-0039-5

Acknowledgments:
Editing and preparing for print Rabbi Yonah Avtzon
layout and typography by Yosef Yitzchok Turner
cover by Avraham Weg

DEDICATION

Dear Guests שי׳,

In honor of our wedding, we are pleased and privileged to present this English edition of זיו השמות — "What's in a Name," composed by our dear brother-in-law, Rabbi Zushe Wilhelm, *Rosh HaYeshiva* and principal of Mesivta Oholei Torah in Crown Heights.

זיו השמות is a unique *sefer*. It is the first literary work of its kind. It is a compilation of the relevant Torah laws and customs devoted exclusively to the time-honored tradition of giving Jewish names to our children.

This project was very dear to our beloved father, הרה״ח הרה״ת ר׳ רפאל משה הכהן שפערלין ז״ל. He was always enthusiastic about this undertaking and encouraged its efforts from the conception of the idea through the publication of the original Hebrew edition. When the first copy came off the press, he would proudly display the manuscript and fervently discuss its subject matter.

Knowing how deeply our father ע״ה, felt about this *sefer*, and how pleased he would be knowing that it is translated into English, we are honored to dedicate this newest edition of זיו השמות, in tribute to his loving memory.

A text highlighting the importance of names serves to emphasize the central significance of the *Mishnah*, "the crown of a good name supercedes them all" (*Pirkei Avos* 4:13). Our dear father ע״ה was favored to enjoy a name of excellent repute during his physical lifetime and ב״ה his sterling qualities are still remembered today. May his good name and great merits help us to be זוכה לבנות בנין עדי עד, על יסודי התורה והמצוה כפי שהם מוארים בתורת החסידות.

Although we continually miss our father's physical presence, it is during family *simchas* that we feel his closeness more than ever. We sense his spiritual influence guiding us and blessing us particularly now, during the celebration of our marriage.

Thank you all for joining us in this festive occasion and may we soon repay your kindness by אי״ה joining together at your *simchas*. Above all, may we all very soon rejoice in the supreme celebration, the revelation of the Rebbe Melech HaMoshiach, and may it be NOW!

Wishing you a כתיבה וחתימה טובה לשנה טובה מתוקה.
יחי אדוננו מורנו ורבנו מלך המשיח לעולם ועד

Ari and Malky Sperlin

Chai Elul 5758
The 300th year since the birth of the Baal Shem Tov
Crown Heights, Brooklyn, New York

TABLE OF CONTENTS

TESTIMONIALS vii
INTRODUCTION ix
   ONE'S MAME IS HIS VITAL FORCE xii
   THE NAME IS THE CAUSE xiii

CHAPTER
1. Who has the right to name a child 1
2. When a boy is to be named 8
3. How and when a girl is to be named 12
4. Naming after parents, or after an event 16
5. Giving a boy a feminine name, and vice versa 18
6. Names common to both males and females 20
7. Names containing the name of G-d 21
8. Naming children after places 23
9. Naming a son after one's Rebbe 25
10. Naming after a living person 27
11. Giving one person two names 30
12. Naming after a former husband 35
13. Naming after a former wife 36
14. Mistakes made while giving the name 37
15. Naming after someone who died young 40
16. Naming a child after someone who died after the child was born 41
17. Naming a child after someone who died, but has not yet been buried 42
18. Naming a child according to the calendar 44
19. Naming a child according to the circumstances of his birth 46
20. Someone whose son or daughter has died (G-d forbid) ... 49
21. Giving two children the same name 51

22. Special objections regarding names..................52
23. Non-Jewish names 53
24. Names predating Avraham *Avinu*......................56
25. "May the name of *reshaim* decay"....................57
26. Naming an adopted child 61
27. Naming a child who died 64
28. Changing a name...66
29. Mentioning the patient's name, and that of his mother, when praying for a sick person 69
30. Calling one's father by his name.......................73
31. Calling one's Rebbe by his name 75
32. Whether a husband and wife should address each other by name......................................77
33. If a second wife has the same name as the first wife........78
34. If a second husband has the same name as the first husband...79
35. A daughter-in-law and mother-in-law with the same name...80
36. A son-in-law and father-in-law with the same name........82
37. *Mechutanim* with the same name....................83
38. *Machutanos* with the same name 85
39. Symbolic reference to the author's name in the title of his *sefer* 87
40. Using titles...89
41. Calling up a person to the Torah by his name...............92
42. Addressing people named Shalom and the like, in the bathhouse...94
43. Miscellaneous 95
44. Reciting a verse beginning and ending with the same letters as one's name....................................96
45. List of verses corresponding to names of men and women..98

TESTIMONIALS

When publishing a work of Torah scholarship, it is customary for the author to show the manuscript to noted rabbinic authorities, and solicit their testimonials approving the printing of the *sefer*. At the beginning of the Hebrew edition of זיו השמות, there appeared testimonials from the following prominent Torah personalities:

R. Yisrael Yitzchak Piekarski ז״ל,
    Rav of Congregation Beis Yaakov, Forest Hills, New York
    Rosh HaYeshivah of Yeshivah Tomchei Temimim Lubavitch

R. Menashe Klein שליט״א,
    Rav of Congregation Ungvar
    Rosh HaYeshivah of Yeshivah Beis Shearim
    Brooklyn, New York

R. Binyamin Yehoshua Zilber שליט״א,
    Bnei Brak

R. Yehudah Hertzl Henkin שליט״א,
    Executive Vice President, *Otzar HaPoskim* Institute

R. Yehudah Kalman Marlow שליט״א,
R. Avraham Osdoba שליט״א,
R. Yosef Avraham *HaLevi* Heller שליט״א,
    Beis Din Tzedek of Crown Heights

לזכות

חמותי מרת **דברא נעכא** תחי'
שפערלין

תרווי הרבה נחת מכל בניך
ויוצאי חלציך שיחיו
מתוך שמחה אמיתית

מלכא דעלמא יברך יתהון,
ויפיש חייהון ויסגא יומיהון,
ויתן ארכא לשניהון

INTRODUCTION

The Jewish name is not merely a means of identifying an individual, but a matter of significance, a concept with spiritual content. Logically, there is a close association between the name and the person bearing it. This is emphasized frequently in the Torah, Prophets, and Holy Scriptures. We see this in *Bereishis* 32:27-28, "He said to him, 'What is your name?' and he said, 'Yaakov.' Then he said, 'No longer shall your name be called Yaakov, but Yisrael, for you have contested with angels and with men, and have prevailed.'" The same concept is stressed several times in the Talmud.

For the above reason, the naming of a Jewish newborn is a sacred undertaking, part of the Jewish religious life cycle. A Jewish boy is named during the *bris* ceremony, as he enters the covenant of Avraham *Avinu*; a girl is named when her father is called up to the Torah.

While it is true that a Jewish boy or girl is named according to the unconstrained joint decision of the parents, this name nonetheless receives its endorsement from Heaven. The name is registered as belonging to this child forever. It is by this name that the boy will be called up to the Torah upon reaching his *bar mitzvah* at the age of thirteen; upon reaching adulthood and marriage, this name will appear in the *kesubah*; this name is mentioned in the *E-l malei rachamim* prayer offered for the benefit of the soul after 120 years. Thus, the Jewish name escorts the Jew throughout life, at all occasions, be they joyful or (G-d forbid) the opposite.

When praying for the speedy recovery of a sick one, and when offering the *mi shebeirach* prayer, the Jewish name is again mentioned, together with the mother's name. When the illness is grave, however, and the patient's life is threatened, the name is often changed, by adding another name to the original one.

This adding of a name is also done within the sphere of the *mi shebeirach* prayer. It is done in *shul*, mentioning the patient's full name, the new and the original together, and beseeching a full recovery in his behalf. This change of name constitutes a sort of change in the patient's identity; this gives rise to the hope that it will likewise alter his fate; *meshaneh shem, meshaneh mazal* — "a change of name brings about a change of fate."

When choosing a name for their newborn child, parents review the names of their dear ones. This is based on the precept of the Torah that the name of the departed shall not be erased from Israel. Occasionally, the child is named after some giant of Torah learning, or the greatest *tzaddik* of the generation, whose life was consecrated to the Torah; or a girl is named after great *tzidkonis* whose life served as an example to the public.

When the child is named after a departed relative — according to Ashkenazic custom — it also fulfills the *mitzvah* of honoring one's father and mother. This *mitzvah* is obligatory not only during their lifetime, but also after their death. It is a great satisfaction to the soul, and affords pleasure to the souls of departed parents, when their descendants bear their names. Especially when the children are fitting members of our people, following the traditions of our forefathers.

Unfortunately, there are many Jewish children who either do not know their Jewish name, or else they are ashamed of it, hiding it behind a non-Jewish name. This is chiefly the fault of the parents, who educate their children in this manner. The Sages have said (*Bamidbar Rabbah* 20:22) that one of the reasons our forefathers merited to be redeemed from Egypt was that they did not change their names — they continued calling themselves Reuven, Shimon, Levi, etc.

Regarding the different categories of Jewish names, they can be classified in general as follows:

i. Biblical names — i.e., names mentioned in the five books of the Torah, in the Prophets, or in the Holy Scriptures;

ii. Talmudic names — i.e., names originally found in the Talmud and *Midrashim*;

iii. names found in Nature — in the animal world, some of which also appear in Scripture, such as Chava, Rachel, Devorah, Tziporah, Yonah, etc. There are also names from the animal kingdom not mentioned in Scripture as names of people, such as Aryeh, Zev, Tzvi; such names originated with the blessings of Yaakov and Moshe, who applied the names of various living things to the Tribes of Israel;

iv. names found in Nature — in the plant world, some of which also appear in Scripture, such as Tamar, etc. Other such names are Shoshana, Alon, Oren, Oranah, Aviva, etc.

v. names that include the Name of G-d within them, and names that express thanks to G-d;

vi. names of Angels, that have been adopted as human names;

vii. secondary names, that occur jointly with the primary name, though occasionally they occur alone.

In this book, we will attempt to collect and elucidate all the laws and customs connected with names of people.

ONE'S NAME IS HIS VITAL FORCE

It is stated in the holy *seforim* that the name by which a person is called constitutes his soul and his vital force. This means that when the soul inhabits the body, it draws life into it by means of the name, i.e., through a correct joining of the letters of the name. It is explained in *Tanya*, ch. 1 of *Shaar HaYichud VehaEmunah*, that for all created things in the universe, the Hebrew name by which they are called constitutes — after progressive stages of evolutionary descent

— the literal speech of the Ten Sayings by which the world was created. This descent occurs through successive exchanges and joinings of the letters in the 231 permutations, until eventually they are embodied within the person to give him life.

The name by which he is called is the vessel that contains the condensed vital force inherent in the letters of the name. As the Holy One said to the Angels, "Adam's wisdom is greater than yours"; for he understood the ultimate source of each created being, and accordingly he called them by their names. Therefore, we find that when we wish to revive someone who has fainted, we call him by his name. By calling his name, we arouse his vital force at its source, and draw vitality down into the body. Similarly, if one is asleep, we call him by his name.

A name has two opposing characteristics. On one hand, the name is associated with the soul. Thus, when we call someone by his name, we arouse his vital force. This applies not only to one's proper name, but also to a descriptive name — when we call someone "wise," we arouse his intellectual faculties; when we call him "merciful," we arouse his pity. Therefore, the disciples of R. Shimon bar Yochai uttered his praises, so that this would arouse their master's great powers, which he would impart to them. All this applies much more so to the proper name, for it arouses not only individual powers, but the entire soul.

On the other hand, it is known that the whole purpose of a name is for the use of others; i.e., so that one's fellow person may call him by it, and he will know that it is him whom he has called. But for himself, a person needs no name; of what use is a name to a person who lives alone? Thus, it appears that the name is not connected with one's essence or vital-force, but is merely established by convention.

The resolution of this paradox is that one's name is like the *sefirah* of *Malchus*; it is but a ray (זיו — **ziv**), that by itself possesses nothing of its own, but is rooted in its original source. For this reason, it has these opposing characteristics.

That one's name represents his vital-force is hinted at by the word *neshamah* ("soul"), whose middle two letters form the word *shem* ("name"). The letters of a person's name are the pipeline through which life is drawn into the body. Therefore, the word שם (*shem*) has the same numeric value as צנר (*tzinor*), "pipe".

THE NAME IS THE CAUSE

The Talmud says (*Berachos* 7b), "How do we know that one's name can cause [events in his life]? Scripture says, 'Go and see the works of the L-rd, Who has put destruction (*shamos*) upon the earth.' Do not read *shamos* שַׁמּוֹת ['destruction'], but *shemos* שֵׁמוֹת ['names']." *Maharsha* explains: we cannot ascribe to the Holy One evil deeds such as destruction, therefore, the Sages interpreted the word *shamos* as *shemos*, meaning that G-d's works are drawn down through a person's name, and thus, the name is the cause.

Again, in the Talmud, we find that R. Meir would make deductions [about a person] from the name, but R. Yehudah and R. Yosse would not deduce anything. Elsewhere, R. Yitzchak declares, "The spies [sent by Moshe to the Land of Israel] had names that reflected their deeds."

The notion that a person's name informs us about his deeds and character, applies not only to individual people, but to the generation as a whole. Thus, the prophet Yermiyahu's name indicates that in his days the *Beis HaMikdash* became *arimon* [vacant], or that in his days severe judgment was *nisromema* [raised up; both of these words share common letters with his name]. This is confirmed in *Zohar*, where Yermiyahu's name (who foretold punishment) is contrasted with that of Yeshayahu, whose name (meaning "G-d's rescue") caused our redemption, and the restoration of the Divine Light to its rightful place.

Sefer Chassidim and *Sefer HaBahir* also caution us about names. *Midrash Tanchuma* comments on the verse, "Remember the days of the world, understand the years of every generation" — one should always examine historical names, and choose for his child a name that will result in his becoming a *tzaddik*.

Thus, we see that a person's name indicates what traits he is likely to possess. From his name, we may guess what sort of person he is, and what his deeds are. R. Yosef Karo writes in *Maggid Meisharim* that a person named Avraham tends to do acts of kindness, a person named Yosef is strong in resisting illicit sexual urges, or else he feeds and sustains others, as did Yosef, who fed and sustained his father and brethren. Scripture says, "Naval is his name, and abomination (*nevala*) goes with him." This is also what Eisav meant when he said, "Is it for nought that his name is called Yaakov? indeed, he has withheld (*vayaakeveini*) from me twice. *Midrash Tanchuma* states that had our generations merited it, the Holy One Himself would have given each individual person his name, and from his name we would thus know his character and deeds.

Zushe Wilhelm

Erev Chai Elul, 5758
The 300th year since the birth of the Baal Shem Tov

CHAPTER ONE

WHO HAS THE RIGHT TO NAME A CHILD

1) Both the father and mother¹ have the right to name their child.²

2) No other person³ (besides the parents) has the right to name the child.⁴

---

1. Yishmael's name was given to him by both Avraham and Hagar; *Bereishis* 16:11,15; *Sifsei Chachamim*, loc. cit.; *Likkutei Sichos*, Vol. 7, p. 308, paragraph 1. (However, no generalization can probably be deduced from this case, since G-d Himself commanded them to give him this name, and that was why they both gave him the same name.)
2. See *Midrash Rabbah, Koheles* 7:3: "A person is called by three names — one is given to him by his father and mother..."; see also *Midrash Tanchuma*, beginning of *Vayakhel*, where the same passage appears in slightly different words.
3. It is written in the writings of the *AriZal:* "When a person is born, and his father and mother give him a name ... the Holy One puts into their mouths the name that belongs to that soul." (Introduction to *Sefer HaGilgulim* 23; *Emek HaMelech*, Part 31, end of ch. 4; *Or HaChayim, Devarim* 29:17). See also *Taamei HaMinhagim* 929, *Kuntres Acharon* quoting *Mishnas Chassidim*; loc. cit., *Kuntres Acharon* quoting R. Michael of Zlotchov, who says that all this applies only when the father (or mother) give the name. But if it is someone else, then the Holy One does not put the name into his mouth. See *Likkutei Sichos*, Vol. 12, p. 182 (quoted in *Teshuvos U'Biurim — Yagdil Torah*, p. 268):
    > Regarding your request for advice on naming your child, my father-in-law's response on this subject is well known — he would not get involved in such matters. We may understand this attitude according to what is written in the writings of the *AriZal*.

    See *Minhagei Komarna* (collected by Avraham Abba Zis) 107:
    > The father of the child would transfer to our Rebbe the rights to all the honors, and the Rebbe would distribute them as he wished. Regarding the blessings after the circumcision, and the giving of the name, many of the celebrants would request that the Rebbe himself give the name, and not honor someone else with this.

3) Regarding which of the two (the father or the mother) has the first right to name their firstborn child — there are differing customs. According to one custom, the right to name the first child belongs to the father,[5] the name of the second child belongs to the mother, and so on, alternately.[6]

See the footnotes, loc. cit.:

> The children of one of the residents of Komarna had all died (may G-d preserve us). Another son was later born to them; at the *bris*, the Rebbe Maharim recited the blessings; when he reached "and may his name be called in Israel...," he said the name silently. Later, he instructed them to call the child Alter, until his *bar mitzvah*. Then, when they would have to call him up to the Torah, they should come to him, and he would reveal the proper name. By the time the child became *bar mitzvah*, the Maharim had passed away. The parents went to Maharash to inquire what name they should now give the boy; Maharash took out a notebook, in which the Rebbe had written the name of the child, in his own handwriting.

4. Even though we find cases where people other than the parents named children. For example, Moshe *Rabbeinu* was named by Pharaoh's daughter (*Shemos* 2:10), G-d having put this name into her mouth; see *Or HaChayim* loc. cit. See *Midrash Rabbah, Vayikra* 1:3: "Moshe was called by six names..."; *Yalkut Shimoni, Shemos* 166:

> His father named him Chever; his mother named him Yekusiel; his sister named him Yered; his brother named him Avi Zanoach; his nurse named him Avi Socho; the Israelites named him Sh'maiyah.

See also *Bava Basra* 15a: "Heiman is Moshe; Moshe was called Mechokek." Thus, we see that Moshe *Rabbeinu* had numerous names. Nevertheless, in the Torah he is called by the name given to him by Pharaoh's daughter (not by the names given by his father and mother). See *Midrash Rabbah* (*Shemos* 1:26):

> This teaches us the reward given to those who do acts of charity: though Moshe had numerous names, the only name used consistently in the Torah is the name he was called by Basya, the daughter of Pharaoh. Even the Holy One Himself did not call him by any other name; (see also *Rus* 4:17).

5. See what the Lubavitcher Rebbe writes in *Likkutei Sichos*, Vol. 7, p. 308, quoted in *Teshuvos U'Biurim — Yagdil Torah*, p. 266 and *Piskei Halachah Uminhag*, p. 114. (He adds that in places where there is no established custom, they should follow this custom.) This is also the ruling of R. Yeshaiyah Gold, in his essay in *Otzros Yerushalayim*, Vols. 14-15. See also *Leket Yosher* (traditions received from the author of *Terumas HaDeshen*), p. 107: "...the custom is that when one's wife gives birth to the first son, he has the right to give the name, and the wife has the right to appoint whomever she chooses as the *kevater*." *Responsa Tashbatz* writes that a grandson was once born to *Ramban*; this child was also a grandson of R. Yonah Geirundi, who had recently passed away. *Ramban* said: "though the proper thing would

WHAT'S IN A NAME? 3

4) Some say that this practice also fulfils the obligation of honoring one's father, if one names his first son after his father (i.e., the child's grandfather). On the other hand, if he fails to

---

be to give the child my name — Moshe — I nevertheless desire that they name him after his grandfather R. Yonah, in keeping with the verse (*Koheles* 1:5), 'the sun shines forth and the sun sets'; thus, the birth of this child will represent 'the sun shines forth' in the same measure that R. Yonah's death represented 'the sun sets.'" From this story about *Ramban*, *Tashbatz* infers that their usual custom was to name the child after the paternal grandfather, not the maternal grandfather. (On the other hand, perhaps we cannot infer that from our story; possibly, their usual custom was to name the child after the *living* grandfather, and this is what *Ramban* meant when he said that the proper thing would be to name the child Moshe.)

We might find a source for the custom in the early commentaries on *Bereishis* 38:5, "And she called his name Shelah, for he [Yehudah] was in Keziv when she gave birth to him." This implies that the custom was for the father to name the first child and the mother named the second child; thus, by right, Yehudah should have named the third child. But it was she who named him ("and *she* called..."); therefore, Scripture had to inform us that Yehudah was away in Keziv when she gave birth, and he was not present to give the name.

Some seek to reject this custom, citing proof from *Ramban's* commentary on the same verse. *Ramban* states that there is no indication here whatsoever for the above-mentioned custom. On first reading, *Ramban's* opinion appears to be that the father has no special right to name the first son. But perhaps he does in fact agree with this custom, and his remarks merely mean that there is no proof for the custom from the present verse.

See *Bris Avos* 8:35, "Regarding the commonly-stated principle that the name given to the firstborn child belongs to the mother, and that she may name the child after a member of her family — in my opinion, there is no basis whatsoever for such a principle. In fact, *Ramban* states just the opposite."

6. We cannot derive this from names mentioned in the Torah, for some of them were given by the Holy One Himself, and others were given by the father. For example, Sheis named his son Enosh; Mesushelach named his son Lemech, and Lemech named his son Noach; Yitzchak named his son Yaakov; Yehudah named his sons Eir, Peretz, and Zerach; Moshe named his son Gershom. On the other hand, some names mentioned in the Torah were given by the mother; e.g., Chava named her sons Kayin and Sheis; Lot's daughters named their sons; Yaakov's wives named their sons.

Some infer from the Talmud (*Kesubos* 106a): "*Rabbeinu HaKadosh* had two sons, Rabban Gamliel and Rabban Shimon; the first was named after [the father's] grandfather, and the second after his father." This implies that the right to name a child belongs to the father. However, it is not definitive proof, for it may be that in this case there simply was no opposition to giving those names, and we can draw no inferences to a case where there is opposition.

name the child after his father it denigrates his honor;[7] this entails a prohibition, and he will be punished for it.[8]

5) Some say that if one gives a name after some member of his father's family (not necessarily after his father himself), this also constitutes honoring his father.[9]

6) Others disagree, saying that only if the parents of the child do not have living parents, they must first name a child after his father (i.e., the child's paternal grandfather), and not after his father-in-law (i.e., the child's maternal grandfather). However, if the child's parents have living parents, then the right to name the first child belongs to the mother's family.[10]

---

7. See *Ikrei Hadat, Yoreh De'ah* 26:7:
    In places where the custom is to name one's first child after his father, if the mother wishes to name him after *her* father, and the husband agrees for the sake of domestic harmony — he may not depart from the accepted custom, for this would denigrate the honor of his father. If she insists, then he should be called by both names, following the custom of some people who give their children multiple names. But he should not belittle his father by naming the first child after his father-in-law, and the second after his father. Perhaps he will not merit to have a second son; and even if he does merit it, it is not fitting to give precedence to the father-in-law's name over the father's name.

    See *Koreis HaBris, Posach Eliyahu* 32, who quotes *Ikrei Hadat*, and comments that if the custom is to name after the wife's father, then we need not be concerned about it.

8. See *Ikrei Hadat*, quoting *Pri HaAretz*, regarding the names Nadav and Avihu. Nadav was named after Aharon's father-in-law, for his wife Elisheva was the daughter of Aminadav; Avihu was named for Aharon's father, i.e. *AviHu* ["my father is he"]. But Aharon was punished for reversing the order of the names. R. Meir Amsel in *HaMaor*, loc. cit. comments that if Aharon sinned, why were his sons punished? Their names caused the punishment. Moshe named his sons after events, and thus did not subject himself to the rule of naming after his father. Aharon, on the other hand, named his sons after ancestors, and thus should have given precedence to his own father. (We still do not understand how Nadav is named after Aminadav, since they are two different names.)

9. See *Responsa Betzeil HaChochmah*, Vol. 3, essay by R. Betzalel Stern, 108:12.

10. See *Otzros Yerushalayim*, op. cit., who infers this from *Divrei Yechezkel* (revised edition), who rules that this right belongs to the mother's family.

WHAT'S IN A NAME? 5

7) According to another custom,[11] the right to name the first child belongs to the mother.[12]

---

11. See *Divrei Yechezkel* (revised edition) by the Shiniver Rav (compiled by R. Yechezkel Shrage Frankel), *Kisvei Kodesh*, nos. 8,9 (pp. 61-62):

    Regarding your request for advice about naming the child, I heard it quoted in the name of the saintly Rebbe of Belz that it ensures long life if the name is given after a member of either the father or mother's family, and the custom is to name the first child after the mother's family, and the second child after the father's family; and so, all the children are to be named in order, one after her family, and one after his family.

    (The substance of these remarks is quoted in *Otzros Yerushalayim*, loc. cit.; *HaMaor*, loc. cit.; and *Eidus LeYisrael*.) See also *Responsa Keser Ephraim* by R. Kasriel Fishel Techurash, ch. 39 (quoted in *Noam*, vol. 13 [5733], p. 295). See also *Shearim Metzuyanim BeHalachah* 163:22; *Nachal Kedumim* on Torah (by the *Chida*), *Shemos* 18:3, quoting Rabbeinu Ephraim, that Gershom the son of Moshe was named by his mother Tziporah. A scriptural hint for this is found in the words *asher shem ha'echad* ["the name of the first one"] — the initial letters for the word *ishah* ["woman"]; Moshe named the second one. (This, however, requires further thought, for a straightforward reading of Scripture implies that Moshe named his son Gershom); see *Sefer HaBris*, loc. cit., where the same idea is expressed; also, *Midrash Rabbah, Shemos* 1:40 implies the opposite of this comment. See the essay by R. Meir Amsel in *HaMaor*, loc. cit., who agrees with this custom. See *Responsa Kol Mevaser* 2:12.

    See *Responsa Igros Moshe, Yoreh De'ah*, part 3, ch. 101; *Responsa Devar Yehoshua* (by R. Yehoshua Menachem Mendel Ahronberg) 2:74.

    We can also cite an actual case in which this custom was followed — when Ms. Hindel, the daughter of the *Chasam Sofer* (wife of R. David Tzvi Ehrenfeld) gave birth to her firstborn son, they informed the *Chasam Sofer* that his first grandson was born. Thereupon, he declared, *Shmuel bekor'ei shemo*, implying that the child was to be named Shmuel, after the *Chasam Sofer*'s father, i.e., after the mother's family. Cf. *Kesov Zos Zikaron*, p. 273 (quoted in *VeYikarei Shemo BeYisrael*, p. 18).

    A primary source for this custom can be inferred from *Yalkut* (*Shmuel*, end of ch. 78):

    A Heavenly Voice would cry out, proclaiming, "a *tzaddik* is going to come forth, whose name will be Shmuel." Therefore, every woman who gave birth to a son would manage to name him Shmuel.

12. Some offer the following reason for this custom: When a woman marries, she abandons her father and mother's home, and is separated from their society and environment. To avoid severing all ties with her family, she is given the right to preserve the memory of her parents by naming the first child after them (*Keser Ephraim*, op. cit.). *Otzros Yerushalayim*, op. cit. offers a different reason: the custom among Torah scholars in almost every Jewish community was that the bride's father obligated himself to support the couple for two years, and so her father was given precedence in naming the first child.

זיו השמות

8) Some have the custom that the name of a daughter belongs to the mother.[13]

9) If a child is given two names,[14] one after his paternal grandfather, and the other after his maternal grandfather, the name of the paternal grandfather should come first.[15]

10) If the child's mother gives him a name, and later, the father arrives and wishes to give him a different name, some say that the father can change the name.[16] Others say that the name given by the mother remains the authentic one, and the father cannot change it.[17] Still others say that the father can add a name, but not change the name completely.[18]

---

13. A *Sephardic* custom cited in *History of the Jews of Baghdad* by R. David Sasson, *p. 185*.
14. See below for the source of the custom to give two names.
15. See *Ikrei Hadat*, op. cit.

   Even when the first son is given two names, the name given after the paternal grandfather should come first. Furthermore, sometimes the use of both names is not maintained, and the child is called only by the first name.

   Accordingly, not only should the name given by the father come first, but they must also call the child by this first name if they wish to call him by one name only.

16. See *Bris Avos:*

   If the father was not present at the circumcision, and the mother named the child; afterwards, the father returned, and rejected this name, wishing to give the child a different name; the question is whether he can legally object or not. We may derive the answer from *Ramban's* commentary on *Parshas Vayishlach* — Rachel named her son Ben Oni ["child of my sorrow"], but "...his father named him Binyamin," ["child of my right hand"], changing sorrow into strength. *Ramban* comments that he really desired to give him the name that his mother gave him, for all his sons were named by their mothers; he merely made an improvement on the name. From the *Ramban* we infer that it was Yaakov only who desired the name given by the mother, knowing that everything they said was by the spirit of prophecy. But if a father rejects the name given by the mother, and is not pleased by it, he certainly may change the child's name.

   He concludes that possibly the name ought not to be changed completely, e.g., from Reuven to Shimon; instead, he should merely alter the name somewhat, as Yaakov did; e.g., from Meshulam to Shalom.

17. See *Nachalas Yaakov, Parshas Shemos*, quoting *Seder Gittin*.
18. See *Responsa Igros Moshe, Yoreh De'ah*, Vol. 3, ch. 97, regarding a case where a son was born; the child's father was not informed, and the mother entered him into the covenant and gave him the name.

However, if they have suppressed the father's name entirely, i.e., they have called the child *"ben ...,"* using the name of a man other than the father, then the name given at the *bris* is null and void, as if the child had been given no name at all.[19]

11) If a girl is born, and her mother gives her a name (through her father — the girl's maternal grandfather — who went up to the Torah and gave her the name), and the child's father is in another place at the time (not knowing that they would give her a name), and he gives her a different name, then the name given by the father is the authentic one.[20]

12) If the first son dies before he is given a name (i.e., before the *bris*), then the right to give a name [to the next child] is retained by the one to whom the right originally belonged.[21]

13) If twins are born, and the one born first is weak, requiring his circumcision to be delayed; and the second child is healthy, and is circumcised on time; then the right to name this second son belongs to the one who has the original right (even though this child was actually born second).[22]

---

19. See ibid.
    ...my opinion is that if the father's name was suppressed completely when the name was given, i.e., they said *"ben ...,"* using the name of some other person; this is a falsehood, and is as if the name had not been given to this child at all, but rather to some other child, the son of an unknown person whom they invented. Thus, it is as if they had not named the child at all at the *bris*. The name that the father gives him will become his real name. But, if they did call him *"ben ..."* using his father's correct name, then the name given at the *bris* is not cancelled; nevertheless, the father can still add an additional name later.
20. See *Responsa Pischa Zuta, Orach Chayim* 45, who so rules.
21. See *Responsa Devar Yehoshua*, Vol. 2, ch. 34: "In my humble opinion, it is clear that this refers not necessarily to the first child, but rather to the first *name*... but since this is the way it generally occurs, he used the term 'first son.'" See also *Responsa Igros Moshe, Yoreh De'ah*, Vol. 3, ch. 101.
22. See *Responsa Igros Moshe*, loc. cit. Note also comment of *Yosef Ometz* (quoted in *Sefer HaBris*, p. 320): "Know, that if in the home where the child was born, there is dissention regarding the name, this poses a danger (G-d forbid) to the child; therefore, it is advisable to consult the mother, so that no conflict will result.

CHAPTER TWO
WHEN A BOY IS TO BE NAMED

1) The subject of what name to give a child should not be discussed before the child is actually born.¹

2) The child's name should not be registered with the office of the civil authorities before the *bris*.²

3) The custom is to name a boy immediately after entering him into the covenant of Avraham *Avinu*.³

---

1. See *Responsa HaMaor*, Vol. 1, p. 134; *Responsa Mevaser Tov* 79. See also *Yerushalmi, Berachos* 1:6:
   > Four people were named before their birth; they were: Yitzchak, Yishmael, Yoshiyahu, and Shlomo. Yitzchak — "And you shall call his name Yitzchak." Yishmael — as is written, "And you shall call his name Yishmael." Yoshiyahu — "For behold, a son shall be born to the House of David, and Yoshiyahu shall be his name." Shlomo — "For Shlomo shall be his name." Thus far, regarding *tzaddikim*. But concerning *reshaim*, "Disperse the wicked ones from the womb."

   See the commentary of *Penei Moshe*: "Thus far regarding *tzaddikim*" — it is only with regard to *tzaddikim* that we find names given before birth. But regarding *reshaim*, "Disperse the wicked ones from the womb," and may their names not be mentioned at all. See also *Mechilta, Parshas Bo*, 16.

2. See *Kovetz Tel Talpios*, Vol. 3, p. 20, the essay by R. A. Karpeles, quoted in *Shaarei Halachah* (by R. Dov Slonim) ch. 202:
   > Question: is it permitted to register the child's name with the office of the civil authorities after birth, before the *bris*?
   >
   > Answer: The name should not be registered before the *bris*, but it is permitted right after the name is announced at the *bris*, or after the mother goes to the synagogue [in the case of a girl; or, after the name is given by the father when he is called up to the Torah, as is the custom]. This is an old custom; see *Responsa Ramam* 34. The source of this custom is in the *Midrash*, at the end of *Parshas Bereishis*, regarding the birth of Noach. See *Alshich* and *Abarbanel*, loc. cit.

3. Scripture nowhere states explicitly when any child was named. Several verses imply that then names were given immediately at birth (see *HaMaor* 5732, no. 2). There is no source for the present custom in the Talmud or *Rambam*. However, a source for our custom is found in several works of the *Rishonim*: see *Zichron Bris LaRishonim, Klalei HaMilah* (by R. Yaakov *HaGozer*), p. 94:

> [At the *bris*, we recite,] "Our G-d, and G-d of our forefathers, preserve this lad for his father and mother, and may his name be called in Israel ... *ben* ..."; this means that while one is blessing the child, he must mention him by name. Another reason why the custom was instituted to name the child immediately following the circumcision is that until then he bore the shameful and unclean name of "uncircumcised"; now that he has been circumcised and the *mitzvah* has been performed upon him, his name must be changed to a praiseworthy one, a pure and holy name like those of his ancestors Avraham, Yitzchak, Yaakov, Reuven, Shimon, Levi, Yehudah, Nasan, Shmuel, Ephraim. The fact that the name is to be changed at the circumcision is deduced from Avraham *Avinu* — before his foreskin was removed, his name was Avram, and he was lacking one letter; immediately after his circumcision his name was changed for the better, and a letter was added to it, naming him Avraham.

The same thing appears in *Migdal Oz*. See also *Mateh Moshe* 3:7:18; *Peirush HaTefillos VehaBerachos* (by R. Yehudah bar Yakar, the Rebbe of *Ramban*), Vol. 2, p. 67:

> "...preserve this lad for his father and mother, and may his name be called in Israel ... *ben* ..." means that we did not wish to give him a name until this point, when he has been circumcised and has become a member of Israel, so that the name will be permanent.

Two reasons are given for this: i) the name that is given to a Jew after he is circumcised remains permanently; thus, we find that Yaakov's original name was not voided [when the name Yisrael was given to him], but the original names of Avraham and Sarah were voided; ii) giving the name while reciting the prayer "preserve this lad..." represents a request that the name be with the consent of the Holy One, and therefore will not have to be changed, as was the case with Yitzchak — the Holy One gave him his name, and thus it was never changed, unlike the case of Avraham and Yaakov.

See the *Siddur* of R. Shlomo of Garmise, p. 287: "Why is a child not named before the day of his circumcision? Because Avraham was not called Avraham until his circumcision." See also commentary of *Dover Shalom* on the *Siddur Otzar HaTefillos* who gives the reason that when the child is circumcised, he reaches his full perfection as a full Jew; then, he may be named according to this attribute of perfection. See also *Pirkei deRabbi Eliezer*, ch. 48: "R. Nesanel says: Moshe's parents saw that his appearance was like an Angel of the L-rd; they circumcised him at the age of eight days and named him Yekusiel." See *Otzar Kol Minhagei Yeshurun*, loc. cit.

The text of *Bereishis* 17:19 reads, "And Avraham called the name of his son who was born to him — that Sarah bore him — Yitzchak"; the next verse says, "And Avraham circumcised his son Yitzchak..." This seems to imply that he was named *before* the circumcision. But we cannot deduce this

4) A child who is born already circumcised is named at the time of *hatafas dam bris*.⁴

5) Regarding a child who cannot be circumcised on time, there are various customs about when to name him. Some say that he is named when his father is called up to the Torah.⁵ Others say that it is better to make it a point to name the child within eight days of birth, before the obligation devolves upon him, and thus, before he can be classified as uncircumcised.⁶ Still others have the custom to delay giving the name until the *bris*, even if it will not be until many weeks later.⁷

6) If the child is a firstborn male, and they are obligated to redeem him, and the *bris* must be delayed; then he is given a name at the time of the *pidyon haben*, and they should not wait until the circumcision.⁸

---

from here, because Avraham had already been instructed by the Holy One what name to give his son; possibly this is why he was named before the circumcision (*Bris Avos* 8:1). Similarly, nothing can be deduced from the case of Rachel who named her son Binyamin on the day he was born, before she died; for it is possible that her prolonged labor lasted for eight days after his head emerged, and thus he was circumcised immediately, and then she died.

4. See *Sefer HaBris*, p. 282, quoting *Midrash Seichel Tov, Parshas Lech Lecha*: "And if he is born circumcised... he is named in the presence of ten men; if ten are not available, he is named in the presence of two."

5. See *Responsa HaMaor*, op. cit.; see also *Responsa Hilel Omeir* 151, quoted in *Kuntres HaShemos* (revised), Vol. 11:

When should a child who cannot be circumcised be given a name? Answer: *Posach Eliyahu* rules that he should be given a name when his father is called up to the Torah. When the name is announced, the soul comes down from the higher world.

See *Koreis HaBris*; however, see *Responsa Teshuvos VeHanhagos* 494.

6. *Chamudei Daniel*, on *Shulchan Aruch Yoreh De'ah*, quoted in *Hilel Omeir*, op. cit.; *Responsa HaMaor*, op. cit. See also *Sefer Asia*, Vol. 4, p. 234ff. It is also mentioned there that it is not good for the child's psychological development to delay giving him a name. See also *Nishmas Avraham (Hilchos Refuah)* p. 174, note 6.

7. See *Sefer HaBris*, p. 282, paragraph 51, who says the same thing, but does not cite a source. See also *Responsa HaShevisas Yom Tov*, Vol. 6, ch. 25.

8. *Pidyon Nefesh*, ch. 5, paragraph 10; quoted in *Searim Metzuyanim BeHalachah* 164:7. See *Edus LeYisrael* (by R. Yaakov Werdyger), p. 200, who casts doubt on this, citing *Chesed LeAvraham* 2:52, stating that a person is classified as

7) If a child is born, and it is necessary to pray for the child's health, then he should be given a name immediately, and then they should pray for him.⁹

---

      human only through the *mitzvah* of circumcision, which is the first step in keeping the Torah.

9. See *Sefer Asia*, p. 249, citing several instances of this rule: there was a sick child whom they wished to pray for, and the Rebbe of Ozorov said (and so said also R. Moshe Feinstein in a similar case) that he must be given a name, even before the *bris*. See *Kfar Chabad* Magazine, No. 322, p. 38 citing a similar story, where the Lubavitcher Rebbe instructed the child's father to send him the name in writing, but not to make it public knowledge until the *bris*.

CHAPTER THREE
HOW AND WHEN A GIRL IS TO BE NAMED

1) Just as a son is named (specifically) by his father, so too, a father names his daughter.¹

2) If a girl is born, and her father is not in town, the daughter should not be given a name until the father returns; he then gives her the name.² Meanwhile, she is called by the family surname.³

3) The father gives his daughter a name when he is called up to the Torah.⁴

4) Among the Sephardim, the ceremony of naming a daughter is called "presentation of the daughter"; their customs in this regard are somewhat different from ours.⁵

---

1. See *Bris Avos* 8:3, "Just as we are particular in the case of males that only their father should give them their name at the *bris*, the same applies to females — at the customary time, the father should verbally declare their names."
2. See op. cit., p. 282, note 3: "It is written in *Yad Aharon, Even HaEzer* 129, that in some families the custom is that if a woman gives birth to a girl, and the husband is not in town, the girl is not named until her father returns."
3. See ibid., "Meanwhile, she is called by the family surname; e.g., if the family name is Ahuvi, she is called Ahavah, and the like. When the father returns, she is given her proper name, Sarah, Rivkah, etc."
4. See *Sefer HaMatamim:* "It is written, 'And you will be called by a new name, which the mouth of G-d shall decide' — the 'mouth of G-d' refers to the Torah." See *Leket HaKemach* (revised edition) 136:28, who rules that calling him up to the Torah for this purpose does not supercede a person obligated to be called up for any other reason, because the name can be given at a later occasion. See *Responsa Minchas Yitzchak*, Vol. 4, 107:1; *Responsa Tzitz Eliezer*, Vol. 14, ch. 21.

5) There are different customs regarding when a girl should be given a name.⁶ Some say that she should be named on the day she is born.⁷

6) Others say that she is given a name on the first opportunity following her birth that the Torah is read. This is done even if it is a weekday; they should not wait until Shabbos.⁸

---

5. See *Siddur Beis Yaakov* (by R. Yaakov Emden) and other Sephard *Siddurim*. This is the procedure for presenting a daughter: the one reciting the blessing takes the child in his arm, and recites:
    My dove is in the crevices of the rock, hidden within the terrace; show me your gaze, let me hear your voice, for your voice is pleasant and your visage is comely (*Shir HaShirim* 2:14).
    (If she is the first daughter, born to him, he adds:
    Unique is she, My dove, My perfect one; she is the only one born to her mother, she is the purest to the one who bore her; daughters have seen her and acclaimed her, queens and concubines have praised her.)
    And they blessed Rivkah, saying to her, "Our sister, may you begat a thousand times ten thousand, and may your seed demolish the gate of their foe."
    Then, the girl is blessed:
    May He who blessed (our foremothers) Sarah, Rivkah, Rachel, Leah, Miriam the Prophetess, Avigayil, and Queen Esther bas Avichayil, bless also this sweet girl, and let her name be called *(... bas ...)*, with good fortune and at a blessed time; may they raise her in health, peace, and tranquillity, and may her father and mother merit to witness her joy and her wedding, children, wealth, and honor; may they come to old age fresh and robust; may this be G-d's will, and let us say *Amein*.
6. See *Bris Avos*, loc. cit., "Regarding women, we are not aware of any especially auspicious time that the Sages have set for naming them. See also *Responsa Minchas Yitzchak*, loc. cit.
7. See *Bris Avos*, loc. cit.
8. See what the Lubavitcher Rebbe writes in *Likkutei Sichos*, Vol. 12, p. 182:
    I was pleased to hear that you named you daughter on Thursday. This accords with what the Rebbe, my saintly father-in-law, related: When one of the Mitteler Rebbe's daughters was born, the Alter Rebbe sent for him and told him: though there is a basis for waiting until the Torah reading of Shabbos to name a daughter, nevertheless — for certain reasons — this should not be done, and the daughter should be named at the first Torah reading following the birth. Since my father-in-law told me about this individual case, it indicates that it is a general ruling for everyone.
    See *Darkei Chayim VeShalom* quoting *Tiferes Banim*, who quotes *Benei Yissasschar* that a girl should be named as soon as possible, at the first Torah

7) Still others have the custom of waiting until Shabbos.⁹

8) Some say that she should not be given a name until five days after her birth; however, if the third day falls on Shabbos, she may be named then.¹⁰

9) Another custom is to wait until the girl is a full month old, and only then do they give her a name.¹¹

10) Others wait until the first Shabbos that the new mother is able to go to the synagogue, and to give the name then.¹²

11) Some wait until forty days elapse before giving her a name.¹³

---

reading following the birth. The reasoning was that whereas when a boy is born, the Torah commands us to wait eight days before circumcising him, and so he is named then; but with a girl, why should we wait even one day before giving her a name in Israel? The name that we give is the soul of the person, and it draws the holiness of Israel into the child; how can we possibly delay this beyond the first day when the Torah is read?

9. See *Responsa Minchas Yitzchak*, Vol. 4, ch. 107, stating that this was the custom in Sighet. See also commentary of *Tosafos Chayim* on *Chayei Adam* 31, that the custom is to give the name on Shabbos, and thus the husband is among those obligated to be called up to the Torah. *Minchas Yitzchak*, loc. cit. gives the reason for this custom: when naming a daughter, it is a bit of a *mitzvah* to rejoice and to prepare a feast. On weekdays people are busy earning their living, and it is difficult to serve a meal with song and praises. Thus, in order to do this *mitzvah* in the best manner, we wait until Shabbos.

10. See *Taamei HaMinhagim* 929: "I heard it said in the name of the holy *tzaddik*, the Rebbe R. Shalom of Belz, that when a girl is born, she should not be given a name before five days have elapsed; but if the third day falls on Shabbos, she may be named on Shabbos." This passage of *Taamei HaMinhagim* is quoted in *Likkutei Sichos*, loc. cit., but it is then questioned: who knows whether this was really said [by the Belzer Rebbe]? *Minchas Yitzchak*, loc. cit. comments that the reason for such a custom is hidden from him.

11. See *Bris Avos* 8:3, "There are places where girls are named at the end of a month after their birth; for women are likened to the moon, and when she has lived for the same number of days as the moon's cycle, she is given a name." *Minchas Yitzchak*, loc. cit. also mentions a custom to wait until two weeks after birth before naming a girl, but he cites no source for this.

12. See *Migdal Oz:* "On the Shabbos when a women who has given birth to a daughter goes to *shul*, the *mi shebeirach* for childbirth is recited, and the girl is named. If she does not go to *shul*, the father (or someone else) gives the name after four weeks, when it is nearly certain that the child is not premature; we are not particular about waiting a full thirty days.

12) A joyous feast is held when a girl is named.[14]

13) When giving a daughter her name, they should be careful to pronounce it correctly, as the name appears in the Torah, and not in diminutive form.[15]

---

13. See *Baalei Bris Avraham, Parshas Toldos,* who states that before forty days the child is not considered born, for the numeric value of ולד ["born child"] equals forty. Just as a boy should not be named until he is circumcised and thus qualified to become the future father of Jewish children, so too a girl should not be named until forty days after birth, when her womb is spiritually qualified to bear future children.
14. See *Taamei HaMinhagim* 1029:
    I have heard that even when naming a daughter there is a bit of a *mitzvah* to rejoice and to prepare a feast, for a holy soul has descended from the higher worlds; the soul arrives when the name is given, for "the soul of a living being is the name." Therefore, the superior individuals who know of this celebrate it as a festival with praises to the Creator. This is what is meant by "who were summoned to the assembly, persons of fame." — they were superior individuals, who celebrated a festival when they named their children, even daughters; though they did nothing else but give the name, they celebrated it as a festival. [A play on words; the phrase "summoned to the assembly" in this verse may also be translated as "calling a festival"; the expression "people of fame" may be translated "men of a name."
15. For example: she should be called "Rachel," and not the diminutive "Rechaleh"; see *Yavetz, Siddur Beis Yaakov* p. 212. The reason for this is so that there will be no confusion about how to write her name in a *kesubah* or a *get*.
    Let us note the words of the *Drishah, Yoreh De'ah* 360, stating that naming a girl is equivalent to a *bris*, and therefore takes precedence over the celebration for a bridegroom:
    Regarding the custom in some places that if — when a bridegroom is led out of the *shul* on Shabbos — there is also a baby girl to be named, the bride and groom are first escorted to where the baby girl is, and from there they proceed to the groom's home. This indicates that they consider the naming of a girl to be the equivalent of naming a boy at the circumcision. The rule is that circumcision takes precedence over a funeral, and a funeral takes precedence over a bridegroom; it thus follows that circumcision takes precedence over a groom's celebration after the wedding ceremony.

Chapter Four
Naming After Parents, or After an Event

1) The original custom was to name a child after an event in the parents' lives — for example, Noach, Yitzchak, Moshe, etc. Later, this custom changed, and children were named after their ancestors.[1]

2) Regarding naming a child after an ancestor: some say that even if the child is given a name that shares only a few letters in common with the name of the ancestor, or even if the names share only a common meaning, the child is considered to have been named after the ancestor.[2]

---

1. See *Midrash Rabbah, Bereishis* 37:
    R. Yosse said: in the old days, people knew their complete pedigrees; therefore, they created names after events. We, however, do not know our complete pedigrees; therefore, we give names after our ancestors. Rabban Shimon ben Gamliel said: in the old days, they knew how to use the spirit of prophecy, and therefore they created names after events. We, however, do not know how to use the spirit of prophecy; therefore, we give names after our ancestors.

    Responsa Ein Yehudah states that this custom was already changed in early Talmudic times. See commentary of *Torah Temimah* on *Bereishis* 37:11, note 4, explaining the above *Midrash:* since we are continually wandering in exile, it is proper for us to bear in mind the lineage of our forefathers, by means of fathers naming their children after their ancestors.

    See *Sefer Matamim*, entry on *Hazkaras Neshamos:* "The reason for the custom that someone whose father and mother are living leaves the *shul* during *hazkaras neshamos* is that children are usually named after those same ancestors whose souls are being mentioned, i.e., the child's grandfather and grandmother. To avoid giving Satan an opening [by mentioning the child's name] while reciting the names of the dead, he should leave the *shul.*"
2. See *Sefer HaBris*, p. 321, ch. 32. See also *Rashi's* commentary on *Yoma* 10a, that there are names in which only a single letter of the original root is preserved.

3) If one has the choice of naming his child after one of two people — one who died recently, and another who died long ago; some hold the custom that the child is to be named after the one who died more recently to the birth of the child.³

---

3. Some cite a proof from the commentary of *Or HaChayim* (on *Parshas Yisro* 18:4), "...and the name of one was Eliezer":

> The meaning of "of one" is that, regarding these names, the reason for this name predated the reason for the name Gershom. First he was saved from Pharaoh's sword, and only then was he a stranger in Midian. The reason why he did not give the name Eliezer first is that he first gave the name after his present circumstance of being in a foreign land, and only then did he seek an earlier event.

CHAPTER FIVE
GIVING A BOY A FEMININE NAME, AND VICE VERSA

1) Some say that one may name a male child after a female.[1] Others maintain that it is better not to convert a feminine name to a masculine one.[2]

---

1. See *Bris Avos* 8:37, "It is customary to name a male child after a woman. For example, if a woman named Dinah passed away, and later a boy is born in that family, he is named Dan; if her name was Brachah, he is named Baruch, etc. This is a good custom, and is quite permissible."
   See also *Koreis HaBris, Posach Eliyahu*, note 8:
   > Only if the mother died right after giving birth do we name the son after his mother, if it is a name common to men and women, such as Brachah or Simchah. But it is not done by changing the name from Tzvi to Tzivyah or from Baruch to Brachah.

   See *Kuntres HaShemos* (revised edition), Vol. 7, p. 10:
   > Question: is it proper to give a male a feminine name, or vice versa; e.g., Sima=Simchah or Aidah=Yidel? Answer: This question arises more often in the Diaspora, where the custom is to give names after deceased parents. Here in *Eretz Yisrael* new names are usually given. See what I wrote previously, quoting *Midrash Rabbah, Parshas Lech Lecha*: "R. Yehoshua be Korcha said: The letter *yud* that the Holy One borrowed from 'Sarai' was divided — half was given to 'Sarah,' and half to 'Avraham.' R. Shimon bar Yochai said: the letter *yud* flew up and came before the Holy One, saying, 'Master of the World: is it because I am the smallest of the letters that you removed me from the name of Sarah the *tzaddekes*?' The Holy One replied, 'Originally, you were in the name of a female, and you were the last letter of her name; now, I will insert you into the name of a male, and you will be the first letter of his name.' And so, it says, 'And Moshe called Hoshea bin Nun Yehoshua.'" This implies that naming a male after a woman represents an elevation of the woman's soul; it also implies that the reverse [naming a female after a man] represents a lowering of the soul.

   See *Sefer HaBris*, p. 313
   > *Sefer HaMetzaref* has just been published; in ch. 3, it states that it is forbidden to give a man a woman's name. But the Sages who preceded

2) It is not proper to name a female after a male.³ Some authorities disagree, and do have a custom of giving a man's names to a female.⁴

---

        us were not concerned about such a thing. We know of many who bore feminine names, such as Rabbeinu Simchah, who was a disciple of *Rashi* and the grandfather of *Ri* of the *Baalei Tosafos*; he was also the author of *Machzor Vitri*.

    See the *Midrash* on *Pinchas* (13:12), where it is related that a certain woman who did acts of charity was named Dinah. After she died, her daughter bore a son, whom she named Dan. It is stated that this elevated her soul from the feminine realm to the masculine realm.

2. See *Sefer HaMetzaref* cited in footnote 1; *Responsa Tzitz Eliezer*, Vol. 11, ch. 56, and references to Vol. 7, 49:13.
3. See *Bris Avos* 8:37,

        Regarding the reverse, naming a woman after a man; for example, if his name was Simchah, and a girl is born to that family; this female must not be named Simchah after him. Or, if his name was Baruch, a girl must not be named Brachah after him ... Giving a male's name to a female constitutes a lowering of the soul of the departed man (G-d forbid). This is especially so in light of what the *kabbalists* wrote, that a person's name represents his soul; it is the inner meaning of the verse, "...each living being [lit., 'living soul'], that is its name." This female would thus acquire a male soul, and be ill equipped to bear children; or, if she does give birth, she will bear no more than a single female child. Only with the help of some very great merit will she be able to bear a male child.

4. See *Responsa HaMaor*, Vol. 1, p. 134, and in *Responsa Mevaser Tov*, stating that this is the custom in America. See *Noam*, Vol. 8, p. 192:

        Question: is it proper to name a female after a deceased male by adding a letter; e.g., Baruch to Brachah? Answer: If there is a possibility of giving this name to a boy, then they certainly should not give the name to a girl. But if no male child is born in this family who can be given the name, then there is no cause for concern. Just the opposite — it is better to give a name after him, even to a girl, than to have no memorial to his name at all.

    See *Devash*, p. 229: The "Rogatchover" was asked about what name to give to a girl born to a certain family; they wished to name her after a departed relative, who had been a man named Shabsi, or Shepsil. They wished to prevent his memory from perishing, and to keep an everlasting memorial to him, and were inquiring how this name might be changed [into a feminine name]. He replied that they should name her Rachel, which means "sheep," and is the equivalent of Shepsil ("little sheep").

Chapter Six
Names Common to Both Males and Females

1) Some say that one should not give his child a name that is common to both males and females.¹

2) Some are particular not to marry a woman whose name is the same as one's own.²

3) If a bridegroom has the same name as his prospective mother-in-law, or if the bride has the same name as her prospective father-in-law, there is no cause for concern, and the bride and groom may marry each other.³

---

1. See *Responsa Divrei Malkiel* 3:75 which states that there are several reasons for concern: fear of the evil eye, and the possibility of causing one to sin. See also *Responsa* of R. Shmuel di Medina, *Even HaEzer* 65, concerning names common to both males and females.
2. See *Maasei Ish, Choshen Mishpat* 7. The inquiry concerns a man and woman who have the same name; he writes that those who are careful to follow the instructions of the *Testament of R. Yehudah HaChassid* should be careful here too, and they should not marry each other. See also *Sdei Chemed*, entry on *Chasan VeKallah* paragraph 7; he writes that he does not find it mentioned in either *Sefer Chassidim* or the *Testament* that one need be particular in this case. If what he means is that this is included in the *Testament of R. Yehudah HaChassid*, then what he is really saying is that one *should* be careful about it, and one of them should change their name. See also *Otzar HaPoskim, Even HaEzer* end of ch. 2, and the *Testament of R. Yehudah HaChassid* 21.
3. See *Shiv'im Temarim* 7, quoted in *Darkei Teshuvah, Yoreh De'ah* 116:50, which states that one need not be concerned here, for *Sefer Chassidim* and the *Testament* mention only the case where a man's name is the same as his father-in-law, or a woman's name is the same as her mother-in-law, unlike the present case. And in fact, we should not add stringencies or seek reasons to be more strict than what is written explicitly in the *Testament*. See *Otzar HaPoskim, Even HaEzer* end of ch. 2, and the *Testament of R. Yehudah HaChassid* 22.

Chapter Seven
Names Containing the Name of G-d

1) In the old days, people preferred to give their children names that contain the Name of G-d, or names that express praise and thanks to G-d. For example, the prefix E-l in the names Elkana, Elchanan, Eliezer, Elazar; the prefix Y-h in the names Yehoshua, Yehoyakim, Yehoyada; the suffix E-l in the names Shmuel, Yerachmiel, Yechezkel; the suffix Y-h in the names Yeshayah, Ovadiah, etc.

2) When writing G-d's name — for example, Elokim — a hyphen should be inserted into the word [E-lohim][1].

3) Regarding names containing the Name of G-d, we are not obligated to insert a hyphen between the letters constituting G-d's Name (e.g., Shmue-l). Nonetheless, some practice an extra degree of piety, and are accustomed to insert a hyphen between the letters *yud-hei* or between the letters *aleph-lamed*.[2]

---

1. See *Responsa Teshuvos VeHanhagos* 638.
2. *Responsum* of R. Simcha Kohen, printed at the end of *El HaMekoros*, Vol. 2, p. 324:
    Question: must I be careful not to throw papers containing my name — Odalyah — into the rubbish, since it includes the Name of G-d? Also — am I required to insert a hyphen between the final two letters of my name?
    Answer: regarding the writing of your name — it is true that the meaning of this name implies thanks to G-d. However, since the word "Odalyah" has now been adopted as your personal name, it has no sanctity at all, and only its lofty significance remains. Therefore, it is not necessary to treat this name as something holy, nor to insert a

זיו השמות

4) For many names, we call the person by the corresponding nickname. For example, Elchanan = Choneh; Eliyahu = Eli; Eliezer = Leizer; Gedalyahu = Gedalia; Yehudah = Yud'l. The reason for this is that these names contain the Name of G-d.³

---

hyphen between the final two letters. The same rule applies to other names, such as Yechezkel, Shmuel; or names of places, such as Beis El.

Despite all the forgoing, some are accustomed to practice an extra degree of piety, and insert a hyphen between the letters *yud-hei* or *aleph-lamed*.

See also *Kovetz Razash*, essay by R. Moshe Wiener.

3. See *Otzar Kol Minhagei Yeshurun* p. 343, paragraph 9; *Taamei HaMinhagim* p. 504, footnote to paragraph 33; *Sefer Matamim* (revised edition), entry on "Name," paragraph 14.

CHAPTER EIGHT
NAMING CHILDREN AFTER PLACES

1) We find in *Tanach* names of people that are identical to names of places. For example: Ephras is the place where Rachel *Imeinu* died and was buried (*Bereishis* 48:7). This name also appears in *I Divrei HaYamim* 2:19, as the name of Calev's wife. Similarly, Edom, the name of a place, is mentioned in *Parshas Toldos* as the name of Esav. There are other similar cases.

2) Nowadays, there are some newly-invented names, used mainly in *Eretz Yisrael*, that are both names of places, and names of people. For example, the masculine names Arnon, Givon, Geva; and the feminine names Kineres, Eilas, Carmella, etc.

3) Some say that one should not give his son two names, one of which is also the name of a place, such as Reuven Chevroni, for this may later result in legal problems.[1]

---

1. *Responsa Kol Mevaser* 2:20:
    Regarding your inquiry about a woman who gave birth to a son, and her husband agreed to name him after a deceased relative of the wife, known as Reuven Chevroni. The husband now refuses; he agrees to the name Reuven, but not Chevroni. You cite the *Gemara*, *Shabbos* 134a: "They named him Nasan HaBavli, after me." But in *Yerushalmi*, *Yevamos* 6:6: the same story of R. Nasan is mentioned, but there the quotation is, "They named him Nasan after me." The same text also appears in *Midrash Rabbah*, *Shir HaShirim* 7 (on the verse "How beautiful are your feet..."), where the word "HaBavli" is omitted. Even regarding the text in our own *Gemara*, we can interpret it to mean that *people* called him Nasan HaBavli, not that he was given this name at birth. We find a similar text at the end of *Yevamos* 122b: "I said to him, 'More power to you, Aryeh ["lion"].' (*Rashi* comments: [he meant to say] 'You are a

mighty warrior, with the heart of a lion'). He replied to me, 'You have correctly guessed my name, Aryeh, for thus I am called in my city, Yochanan ben Yonasan, Aryeh of Kefar Shichaya.'" Another example is found in scripture, *Parshas Toldos:* "For this reason, he was named Edom" (though at birth he had been named Esav, his proper name).

See commentary of *Ramban*, loc. cit. It is also evident that the text in *Yerushalmi* and *Midrash Rabbah* is the correct one (i.e., the child was named Nasan only). Even in the case of Yaakov *Avinu*, we do not find him to have the two names Yaakov and Yisrael at the same time. Nor do we find anywhere among the names mentioned in *Tanach*, the Talmud, or the *Poskim*, one person having two names at the same time. This also appears to be what *Yam Shel Shlomo* writes on *Gittin* 4:26, regarding a case where the father wished to name his son Meir, after his own father, while the mother wished to name him Uri, after her father. They named him Schneur, meaning two sorts of light, Meir and Uri. Now this is difficult to understand, for they ought to have named him Meir Uri, unless in those days the custom [of giving one person two names] had not yet arisen. *Nachalas Shivah* also comments that he found it strange when people had two names at once. This implies that in the old days this was not common. See also *Rama, Even HaEzer* 129:14.

In our days, the custom has become widespread to give two names at once, when a child is born; i.e., both are proper names (not that one is a proper name, and the other a descriptive name). Nevertheless, it is better, from a legal standpoint, not to do this, for there is the danger that it will cause problems regarding a *get* — if he were to get divorced, and his name were written Nasan HaBavli, or Reuven Chevroni, it would imply that this person was born (or lived) in Bavel, and the other person was born (or lived) in Chevron. (See *Kiddushin* 76b: "But what about Tzelek *HaAmoni*; does this name not imply that he *was born* in Amon? No, it may imply that he *lived* in Amon. And what about Uriah *HaChiti?* Does this name not imply that he *was born* in Cheis" No, it may imply that he *lived* in Cheis.) These implications are contrary to fact, and thus the name of his place has been altered, thus disqualifying the *get*, as stated in *Even HaEzer* 128.

CHAPTER NINE
NAMING A SON AFTER ONE'S REBBE

1) It is proper to name a son after one's Rebbe.[1]

2) Some say that naming after one's Rebbe takes precedence over naming after one's ancestor.[2] Others dispute

---

1. The reason is that this is a form of honoring one's Rebbe. See *Bris Olam* p. 231, and *Avos deRabbi Nasan* 15:3:
   > It is said that two sons were born to that convert; one was called Hillel, and the other was called Gamliel. Both were referred to as "Hillel's Converts."

   See also *Shabbos* 134a, concerning Nasan HaBavli; women whose sons had died as a result of circumcision came before him. He instructed them to wait [before circumcising future children] until they would grow stronger. They took his advice, and they also named the sons after him Nasan HaBavli. See also *Avos deRabbi Nasan* 12:4 — there were thousands of Jews who were named Aharon; for were it not for Aharon, they would not have been born. Aharon would restore harmony between husbands and wives; thereafter, they would have relations, and name the resulting child after him. See also *Bava Metzia* 84b concerning R. Eliezer ben R. Shimon — when he arrived at the *beis hamedrash*, sixty specimens of blood were brought before him; he declared all of them to be clean, and permitted the women to have relations with their husbands without prior immersion. All of them gave birth to male children, and they were named Eliezer after him. Thus, we find several passages by the Sages that describe people naming their sons after their Rebbe. See also *Noam Elimelech* on *Bamidbar*.

2. See *Chemda Genuza* Part 1, quoted in *Sefer HaBris* p. 320 — for this reason, Ramban instructed his son R. Shlomo to name his son after R. Yonah, who was the child's maternal grandfather. According to custom, the child should have been named after his paternal grandfather; nevertheless, this was done because honoring one's Rebbe takes precedence over honoring one's father. This is supported by the *Gemara Bava Metzia* 33a, "returning a lost object to one's Rebbe takes precedence over the lost object of one's father."

   On a related theme, is the story (regarding the Alter Rebbe's son, Reb Chayim Avraham) related in *Sefer HaMaamarim 5709*, p. 90, also quoted in *Toras Shmuel*, Vol. 2, p. 617:

this, saying that naming after one's ancestors takes precedence over naming after his Rebbe.[3]

When my uncle R. Avraham was three years old, he became deathly ill. His father summoned a *minyan* of ten *bochurim* who were his students, and four local residents, including Reb Gavriel and Reb Nachman...

... When they entered, he told them that during the previous night his Rebbe had appeared to him. He had asked him why he failed to beseech mercy in behalf of his son, the sick child, who carried his name.

He replied that the source of the illness was the complaint by his grandfather — his father's father-in-law — whose name was incidental, and thus not known publicly.

"I told my Rebbe that I had acted properly; where there is a choice between honoring one's Rebbe and honoring one's father (especially when it is only one's grandfather), **the honor of one's Rebbe takes precedence**. This applies especially to giving names. Since it serves to reveal the illumination of the soul, and its assimilation into the soul of the one receiving the name, it follows **that the Rebbe's name takes precedence over the father's name**.

"Now, I have discovered that my maternal grandfather's name was Chayim Avraham. Therefore, I have summoned you to join me in changing the child's name from Avraham ben Sterna to Chayim Avraham ben Sterna. May G-d (blessed be He) send him a recovery, may he become a chassid and a Torah scholar, and may G-d grant him long life."

My uncle Reb Chayim Avraham recovered, and became a healthy child.

See *Siach Sarfei Kodesh*, before Part 5, p. 48, section 14:

I heard that the Rebbe of Sochatchov told a story about the father of the *gaon* R. Yisrael Yehoshua of Kutna. When this genius child was born to him, he had planned to name him after the Baal Shem Tov, and he also desired to name his son after the author of *Penei Yehoshua*, whose name was Yehoshua, and he also wished to name him Eliyahu, after the *Gaon* R. Eliyahu of Vilna. But the Holy One put words into his mouth, and he called the child Yisrael Yehoshua, which includes all three names — the names Yisrael and Yehoshua are explicit, and the name Eliyahu is implied between them: Yisrael ends with the letters *aleph lamed*, and Yehoshua begins with the letters *yud hei vav*; together, these letters spell Eliyahu. From this story, we see that giving a name involves a minor prophecy.

3. See *Responsa Mishneh Halachos* (by the *Gaon* R. Menashe Klein) 6:252 and 6:258, quoting a letter by the *Gaon*, author of *Machane Chayim*. See also R. Klein's remarks printed at the beginning of the Hebrew edition of this book.

CHAPTER TEN
NAMING AFTER A LIVING PERSON

1) The custom among Ashkenazim is not to name a child after a person who is still living,[1] even if that person lives in another country.[2] Some say that the objection is specifically to naming after one's *father* who is still living, but there is no objection to naming after other living relatives.[3]

2) The custom among Sephardim is not to be particular about this. On the contrary, they consider it to be a form of

---

1. See *Sefer Chassidim* 460, and the comment of *Mekor Chesed*, loc. cit. Also, *Sedei Chemed*, section on *Chasan VeKallah*, subsection 5, the passage beginning, "and our master the *Chida*...." *Bris Avos* quotes R. Shlomo Aharon Wertheimer, who says that when the *Chida* discovered that a child had been named after a living grandfather, he thought it strange.

   When my son was born, it was my idea to name him Menachem Mendel. Since my wife's grandfather (who was then still living) was named Yaakov Menachem Mendel, I asked the opinion of the *Gaon* R. Zalman Shimon Dworkin a.h. whether I could still name my son Menachem Mendel.

   R. Dworkin replied that there were several grounds for ruling leniently here: i) the grandfather had an additional name; ii) the grandfather was not usually called Menachem Mendel, but only Yaakov. These reasons notwithstanding, the whole subject is based on personal objections, and therefore it would be better to refrain from doing something that people usually object to.
2. *Otzar Kol Minhagei Yeshurun*, loc. cit.
3. See *Likkutei Sichos* Vol. 17, p. 474:

   Regarding what is written in *Sefer Chassidim* 600 — from a straightforward reading of the text, it appears that he is referring exclusively to naming a son after one's living *father*.

honoring one's father, and a protective charm for long life, if a grandchild is named after a living grandparent.⁴

3) Most authorities agree that one should not give his son the same name as his own.⁵ However, among the Yemenites, some do have the custom of giving children the same name as their own.⁶

4) If the child's maternal grandfather requests that his grandson be given his name while he is alive, there is no reason to forbid it.⁷

5) If one desires to name his son after his deceased father, but his stepfather — who has the same name — strongly objects, then he should not name the son after his father alone, but should add another name to it, and call the son by both names.⁸

6) If the child's paternal grandfather and his maternal grandfather have the same name,⁹ and one of them has died, and [the father] wishes to name the child after the deceased grandfather — if the surviving grandfather objects, then it is

---

4. See comment of *Mekor Chesed* on *Sefer Chassidim*, loc. cit.; *Sefer HaBris*, p. 315; *Sicha* of the Lubavitcher Rebbe, Shabbos *Parshas Mikeitz* 5743, paragraph 43.
5. Comment of *Bris Olam* on *Sefer Chassidim*, loc. cit.; *Responsa Chelkas Yaakov* 2:120. The reason for this is to avoid infringing on the father's honor — i.e., if this father has more children, they would be unable to address the first child by his name, for it would be the same name as their father.
6. See *Even Sapir* by R. Meir Sapir, who describes such a Yemenite custom. In particular, in families where children have died, their custom is that when another son is born, he is named after his father. See also *Bris Olam*, loc. cit.; *Mekor Chesed*, loc. cit., and references cited there.
7. *Noheg KaTzon Yosef*, section on childbirth, subsection 5, describing the case of a person who had an only daughter, and no sons. While he still lived, his daughter gave birth to a son, and he requested that the son be given his name, and after a hundred and twenty years this son should say *Kaddish* after him. And so she did. It is not forbidden in such a case, for the whole purpose of the custom is to avoid a quarrel, and so that the father will not claim that they are anticipating his death. But here, since he himself is not particular about it, there is no problem.
8. *Responsa Chasan Sofer* 84.
9. See below, Ch. 37.

better to refrain from doing this, since most people would object to it. However, if the deceased grandfather had a nickname, the grandson should be called by this nickname. When the other grandfather passes away following a long life, they may then call the child by the original name also.[10] Or else, they may change the grandson's name slightly,[11] or give the grandson an additional name to be used together with the grandfather's name.[12]

7) A person who is in the process of dying (*goses*) is considered to be fully alive in this regard (even though most such people do die). A child should not be named after him until he has actually died.[13]

---

10. *Responsa Zichron Yehudah* 126.
11. See comment of *Beis Shmuel* on *Even HaEzer* 129, list of men's names beginning with *aleph*, entry for "Avraham," quoting *Maharshal:*
    > It may happen that one's father is living, and named Avraham, while his father-in-law — whose name was also Avraham — is deceased; if he wishes to name the son after [the deceased grandfather], he should name him Avram.

    See also the list of women's names, entry for "Esther," on the same subject.
12. *Responsa Chelkas Yaakov* 2:120.
13. Such a case occurred with R. Shlomo Kluger — when he arrived in Brody, he was honored to be a *sandek*. The child's father was in the process of dying, and the people of Brody said that in such a case it was their custom to wait [until the father died], and to name the child after his father. But R. Shlomo Kluger insisted that they hurry to enter the child into the covenant of Avraham Avinu. Thereupon, the father immediately felt better, and eventually recovered. See *Beis Yisrael* (1st edition), p. 14; (2nd edition), Part 1, p. 78.

CHAPTER ELEVEN
GIVING ONE PERSON TWO NAMES

1) Nowhere in the Talmud do we find a *Tanna* or *Amora* who is called by two names. Even in the Biblical texts we do not find one person called by two names.[1] Nevertheless, these

---

1. See *Responsa Noda BiYehudah* (2nd edition), *Orach Chayim* 113:
   To the best of my recollection, I am unaware of any *Tanna* or *Amora* mentioned anywhere in the Talmud who was called by two names where both were proper names, except Abba Shaul and Abba Yosse. Even here, they are not really two names; in my opinion, Abba is not a proper name, but rather a title of importance. See *Berachos* 16b. I believe that it was not the custom to have two names. Even in Scripture, two names is not very common. See *Pesachim* 117a and *Chulin* 65a. But in the days of the *Tannaim* and *Amoraim* it was not done at all.

   See also ibid., where he explains that when we find in several places in the Talmud the name Biribi joined with another name (e.g., R. Oshiya Biribi, R. Eliezer HaKapar Biribi), we assume that Biribi is a title indicating that he was the greatest of his generation; we do not say that he had two names. However, when Biribi is mentioned by itself (*Chulin* 52b, *Makkos* 5b), we cannot understand it to mean "Biribi (the greatest of the generation) said such and such...," since the text ought to be explicit, and instead it is ambiguous, for we do not know to whom this refers or to which generation it refers. In every generation there are numerous great sages. Therefore, *Rashi* explains that [Biribi] here is the name of a sage.

   See also *Responsa Chasam Sofer*, *Even HaEzer* 2:18:
   It also seems to me that in the old days it was not customary to give two names together; this is a modern innovation. Even in the case of Yaakov Avinu, we do not find that he was called Yaakov Yisrael, using both names at once. Nowhere in *Tanach*, the Talmud, or the *Poskim* do we find anyone called by two names at the same time. Regarding the passage at the end of *Yevamos*, "Thus I am called in my city, Yochanan be Yonasan Arye" — I believe that Arye is not a proper name at all, but rather a family surname indicating that they were powerful, and that both father and son were called Arye. Apparent exceptions are Abba Shaul, Abba Yudin, and Abba Guryan, where Abba appears to be an independent name. However, since we find this only where Abba is the

days it is common to give more than one name to the same child. Others object to giving one child two names, even in our days.²

2) A single name may be composed of two names; for example, Schnei Or³ and Shem Tov.⁴

---

accessory name, I believe that the two form a single name, similar to "Pedah-Tzur" and "Gamli-El"; Abba-Yudin means "The Greatest of the Jews." *Yam Shel Shlomo* appears to say the same thing, citing a case of a father who wished to name his son Meir, after his own father; the mother wished to name him Uri, after her father. The result was that they gave him the novel name Schneur, meaning two different lights derived from both Meir and Uri [both meaning "light"]. Now we wonder why he could not have been named Meir Yair; thus we are forced to conclude that such was not customary in those days. Similarly, *Nachalas Shivah* expresses wonder at people who had two names at once, implying that this was not done in the old days. See *Rama* on 129:14; *Get Pashut* 100:3, stating that the name ShemTov is composed of the names Shem (son of Noach) and Tov (the redeemer of Ruth). However, see *Responsa Mishneh Halachos*, Vol.5, ch. 215, and Vol. 6, ch. 255.

2. See *Responsa Teshuvos VeHanhagos* 606.
3. See what the Maharshal writes in *Yam Shel Shlomo*, Gittin 4:26 at the end:

I too, know of the case of my grandfather R. Menachem Tzion; his father's name was R. Meir, and his father-in-law's name was R. Uri. When he had a son, there was a dispute over which name the son should be given. In the end, he was called Schne-Or, meaning "two lights," for Meir means light , and Uri means light.

See also *Tiv Gittin*, in the list of male names beginning with the letter *shin*, entry for Schneur:

It is also clear that the sage who wrote the above regarding the name Schneur did not mean to say that this name was invented then. What he meant was that sometimes a name is given to effect a compromise in a dispute between husband and wife. As in our case, where the *rav* suggested the compromise of giving a name composed of both names. Similarly, a compromise is sometimes effected by one giving the Jewish name, and the other giving the secular name. In any case, the name Schneur was not invented then, but had existed previously. This is clear, for the sage who wrote this was apparently a disciple of *Maharil* (or of one of his disciples); he writes about his grandfather R. Menachem Tzion, who lived at the time of *Maharil*. The name Schneur is found in very old texts; in *Chidushei Ramban* and subsequent works, a R. Meir ben R. Schneur is mentioned. Thus, the name was not made up for the above-mentioned event.

(The *Maharshal* that the *Chasam Sofer* cites to prove that even in his days they would not give two names requires further investigation, for it states that the child's father was named Menachem Tzion, and so he had two

3) Occasionally, a child is given a proper name after one person, and a nickname (secondary name) after another person, even when the nickname bears no relation to the proper name.[5]

4) If a person becomes seriously ill, he is given an additional name.[6]

5) If one's earlier sons died as a result of circumcision, and then another son is born to him, some are accustomed to give this son two names.[7]

6) Some say that the names of two different people should not be combined and given to a single child.[8] Others are not particular about it.[9]

---

names. It thus appears that *Maharshal* is speaking only of the origin of the name Schneur.)

4. See *Get Pashut*, letter *shin*, subsection 63: "Shem-Tov is a combination of the two names Shem (the son of Noach) and Tov (the one who was supposed to redeem the property of Rus)."

5. See *Yam Shel Shlomo*, loc. cit.

Maharil was asked why sometimes a Yiddish name has many variations in Hebrew. For example, [the Yiddish name] Zalman is associated with the Hebrew names Shlomo, Yekusiel, Meshulam, Shmaryah, and many others. He replied that every Yiddish name certainly has an official Hebrew equivalent. But sometimes, the husband and wife disagree on naming their son, each one desiring to name him after a member of their own family. Occasionally, a compromise is reached, whereby the Yiddish name is from the woman's family, and the Hebrew name is from the husband's family (or vice versa).

6. See *Rosh HaShanah* 16b:

R. Yitzchak said: four things annul an adverse judgment against a person; they are: charity, prayer, changing his name, and changing his deeds.... Changing his name — as it is written, "Your wife Sarai's name shall no longer be called Sarai, for Sarah shall be her name." Thereafter is written, "And I will bless her, and I will also give to you a son through her." See below, ch. 28.

7. See *Atayos Eliyahu*, p. 34, note 51, quoting *Radal*; also quoted in *Darkei Teshuvah*, *Yoreh De'ah* 116:48. See also below, ch. 20.

8. See *Bris Avos* 8: 39:

I heard from my father *Shlita*, that he heard from the holy Rebbe, *Mahara* of Stretyn, that one should not combine the names of two people to give to a child. This is strange, for the common custom is not so, and people do combine the names of two people. Also, *Ikrei Hadat*, *Hilchos Kibbud Av VaEm* implies that it is permissible to do this; he writes that to maintain domestic peace, one may name his firstborn son

WHAT'S IN A NAME?

7) One child should not be given the combined names of two people who feuded with each other during their lifetime, even if both of them were *tzaddikim*.[10]

8) Some say that one should not give his son the combined names of his father and his brother (the child's uncle), but that he should give the child his father's name only.[11]

9) Some say that one should not give his son the combined names of his father and his father-in-law, but only the name of his father.[12] Others dispute this.[13]

10) One should not combine the name of a family member with the name of a Rebbe.[14]

11) If a child is given two names after two different people, it is proper to call him by both names.[15]

12) If one's parents are still living, and have two names, there is no objection to giving his son or daughter one of the

---

after both his father and his father-in-law, combining the two names. Possibly our masters intent was to forbid combining the names of two different people where one was a *tzaddik*, and the other an ordinary person; but combining the names of two ordinary people is permitted. And in the case of two *tzaddikim*, it is certainly a good thing, and it is proper to do so, for the merits of the two *tzaddikim* will protect the child, so that he may live well. But, if the two people quarreled while living, then even if they were both *tzaddikim*, their names should not be combined. See also *Shem HaGedolim* by *Chida*, entry on *Gedolim*, letter *shin*, in the addendum on the name Schneur; analyze this carefully.

9. See *Ikrei Hadat*, Yoreh De'ah 26:7, quoted above.
10. *Bris Avos*, loc. cit.
11. *Responsa BeTzeil HaChochmah*, Vol. 1, ch. 34.
12. *Response Beer Moshe*, Vol. 1, ch. 60, paragraph 2; *Responsa BeTzeil HaChochmah*, Vol. 1, ch. 34.
13. *Ikrei Hadat*, loc. cit.
14. See *Yagdil Torah*, New York, Nisan-Iyar 5743:
    In response to your question regarding naming your son, and your decision to name him after his grandfather, Yechiel Dov; and when adding the name Dov, it is your intention that this is the name of my saintly father, o.b.m. — Do not do this, and do not have such intent in mind, for we do not mingle what is holy with what is not holy.
15. Otherwise, the second name becomes a forgotten name. See *Ikrei Hadat*, Yoreh De'ah 26:7 where this is implied. See also *Responsa Teshuvos VeHanhagos* 608.

two names. The same applies to the opposite case — i.e., he wishes to give his child two names, and the parent has only one of the names.[16]

---

16. For example: if her mother's name is Chaya Sarah, there is no objection to calling her daughter Sarah alone, for this is a different name (see *R. Akiva VeToraso, Yalkut Igros* 16).

CHAPTER TWELVE
NAMING AFTER A FORMER HUSBAND

1) If a woman has a son through her second husband, she should not name him after her first husband if the second husband objects to it.[1]

---

1. *Responsa Asei Lecha Rav* 1:45:
    It is explained in the *Halachic* literature that a second marriage completely annuls the former relationship. It is not proper to display any signs of mourning for the first husband in the second husband's presence. The husband too, is not permitted to display signs of mourning for his first wife in the second wife's presence. Even visiting the grave of a former spouse is forbidden if the present spouse objects. The basis of this rule lies in the disharmony that would result if one were to display a continuing personal relationship with a former spouse, whereas all the ways of Torah are "ways of pleasantness, and all its paths are peace."

    Regarding your particular case, you should very cautiously ask your husband whether he would object to your naming your son (assuming that the child to be born will be a son) after your deceased husband. If he willingly (and with no coercion at all) gives his assent, then only in such case may it be done. But if he is opposed to it, he is within his rights.

Chapter Thirteen
Naming After a Former Wife

1) If one has a daughter born to him through his second wife, some customs would permit him to name the daughter after his first wife.[1] But this applies only if the second wife does not object to it.[2]

---

1. *Segulas Yisrael*, section on "Names," 82:
    Regarding the custom of giving a daughter born of a second wife a name after one's deceased first wife: this is supported by the commentators (see *Rashi*) on the verses in *Divrei HaYamim I* 2:18-19, "Calev ben Chetzron begat Azuvah"; they write that Calev had a deceased wife whose name had been Azuvah, and so, he named his daughter Azuvah. It is written, "Azuvah died, and Calev took unto himself Efras." From this, we learn that he had once had a wife named Azuvah (*Nefesh HaYafah*).
2. *Responsa Asei Lecha Rav* 1:45; see also ibid. 3:34, regarding mentioning the name of one's former wife when reciting the prayers for departed relatives.

CHAPTER FOURTEEN
MISTAKES MADE WHILE GIVING THE NAME

1) If someone has in mind a certain name to be given to his son, but while the blessing ("preserve this lad ...") is being said, when the one reciting the blessing reaches the passage "and may his name be called in Israel ..." the father specifies a different name from the one he had in mind, the son should remain with this different name.[1]

2) If the one reciting the blessing gives a name that is different from the one that the father instructed him to say, we need not worry about it; the son should remain with only the name specified by the father.[2]

3) If one names his son after a deceased relative, and it is later discovered that the relative is in fact still living, we need not worry about this departure from the usual custom of not naming after living people, since when the name was originally

---

1. See *Bris Avos*, quoted in *Bris Olam*, p. 229; *Responsa Mevaser Tov* 79.
2. See *Responsa Maharam Brisk*, Vol. 2, ch. 7, quoted in *Sefer HaBris*, p. 320, paragraph 31:
    Regarding one reciting the blessings after the circumcision, who mistakenly gave the child a name different from the one the child's father instructed him to give; i.e., the father instructed him to name the child Yisrael Aryeh, and the one saying the blessings said Naftali Aryeh. In my opinion, it is obvious that the following should be done — the child's parents should suppress the name Naftali, and call him Yisrael Aryeh. To reinforce this, whenever the father is called up to the Torah, he should have a *Mi Shebeirach* recited for the child, saying, "... and let his name be called in Israel Yisrael Aryeh...." Naming a male child has no real connection with the *mitzvah* of circumcision; it is only that the custom has arisen not to name the child until after the circumcision.

given, they were unaware that he was alive.³ Some say, that they should add an additional name, but not remove the original name.⁴ Others add that if the family objects, then they may even remove the original name.⁵

4) If a child has been given two names, and afterwards they remember that the child's grandfather bears one of these two names, then the child should not be called by this name, but only by his second name. This also applies to the English name — he should not be called by that name.⁶

5) If an additional name has been given to a sick woman, and it is later discovered that this added name is the name of

---

3. See *Likkutei Sichos*, Vol. 17, p. 474:
    It would seem that since the person asking this question intended to give the name after a deceased living person rather than a living person, it does not constitute a departure from Jewish custom; especially since he was unaware that there was a living grandmother with this name. Thus, we are left only with your concern about people who are particular about it, or are worried about giving Satan an opening. Similarly, a straightforward reading of the text of *Sefer Chassidim* indicates that he speaks only about naming after one's *father* who is living.
4. See *Responsa Yad Eliezer* ch. 111.
    Regarding someone who named his son at the *bris* with the same name as his paternal grandfather. The grandfather was very angry, deeming this to be a denigration of his honor. The son offered the excuse that he had done it unwittingly. The question now is whether it is proper to change the name now, at the *pidyon haben*, since the name originally given has not yet been in use for thirty days.
    Reply: it is permitted to change the child's name, for the sake of peace. But the original name should not be removed completely; it should be used in conjunction to the principle name, which is the new name given now.
5. See *Responsa Beis Naftali* 23; *Darkei Teshuvah* 115:48; *Responsa Pri HaSadeh* Vol. 3, ch. 7.
6. See *Likkutei Sichos*, Vol. 17, p. 474:
    What you write is somewhat strange, regarding the grandson of Shalom Moshe HaKohen being named Yosef Moshe. Possibly, there is a typographical error here. Or perhaps, the grandfather's name Moshe is a name that has been suppressed. If this is not the case, then it would be worthwhile — without calling undue attention to it — to try to arrange that the grandson's principle name should be Yosef. This is also with regard to his English name.

her sister, then even if thirty days have elapsed, they should add yet another name, and this name should be kept.[7]

---

7. See ibid.:
> You ask my opinion about having added a name to a certain woman, because she was sick; thereafter, they remembered that the added name was also her sister's name. I wonder why you do not mention whether thirty days have already passed since the added name has been in use? In any case, my opinion is that things should not be done that appear strange, as written in several sources, particularly the *Testament of R. Yehudah HaChassid*. Thus, even if thirty days have already passed, they should follow the ruling regarding a name that has been suppressed, and they should add a new name. This should be done, as is customary, with a *mi shebeirach* when a relative is called up to the Torah. This name should be kept. As is written in several sources, the new name should come first.

Chapter Fifteen
Naming After Someone Who Died Young

1) One should not give a name after someone who died young.[1] In such a case, they should add another name to his name,[2] and the added name should be used as the first name. Some say that one who died before the age of fifty is considered to have died young. Others say that one who died before the age of sixty is considered to have died young.[3]

2) This rule does not apply to one who died a natural death. Even if he was young, not old, a child may be named after him.[4]

3) Even a person who died a natural death, if he died childless, a child should not be named after him.[5]

4) If a *tzaddik* was assassinated at a young age, some say that we may nevertheless name a child after him, in view of the fact that he was a *tzaddik*.[6]

---

1. The reason is that the name causes bad luck. See *Yam Shel Shlomo* on *Gittin*, ch. 4, paragraph 31, regarding the name Yeshayah: "although the Prophet Yeshayahu was called Yeshayahu, people do not commonly name children after this prophet, for it causes bad luck, since he was assassinated." See also *Beis Shmuel*, *Hilchos Gittin*, list of masculine names, letter *yud*; *Responsa Adnei Paz*, quoted in *Pischei Teshuvah* 116:6.
2. See *Minchas Elazar*, Vol. 4, ch. 27; *Darkei Chayim VeShalom*, addenda, paragraph 929.
3. Quoted in the name of R. Yaakov Kamenetzky.
4. *Responsa Igros Moshe, Yoreh De'ah*, Vol. 2, ch. 122, rules that only if he was murdered is the name considered to bring bad luck; but the natural lifespan that G-d allots to a person is not to be considered a curse (G-d forbid).
5. *Responsa Igros Moshe*, loc. cit.; for if someone dies childless, it is probable that this is because of his sins. Thus, this is his punishment, and constitutes bad luck.
6. *Responsa Igros Moshe*, loc. cit., inferred from the text of *Rama, Even HaEzer* 129:26, stating that one may use the name Gedalyahu, even though he was assassinated, because he was a *tzaddik*.

Chapter Sixteen
Naming a Child After Someone who Died After the Child was Born

1) One may name a child after someone who died after the child was born.¹

2) An orphan who is born after his father has died, should be named after his father.²

---

1. See *Responsa Teshuras Shai* (1st edition), 630:
    Regarding the question of a male child who is born, and the father (or someone else) dies before the circumcision, whether it is proper to name the child after the deceased: I heard a ruling in the name of a certain *rav* (who was asked this same question) that they should not name the child after the deceased. But in my opinion, it is proper to name him after the deceased, as implied in *Moed Katan*, ch. *VeEilu Megalchin* 25b.
   See also *Responsa Mishneh Halachos* Vol. 4, end of ch. 152.
2. See *Moed Katan* 25b:
    Rav Chanin had no children. He prayed for mercy, and then he had [a child]. On the day that he was born (and needed to be circumcised), he passed away. The one delivering the eulogy began: "Joy was changed to anguish, rejoicing and sorrow were joined together, at the time of his happiness he lamented, at the time of his favor, favor was lost." They then added the name Chanan ["favor"] to his name.
    See also *Agudah* on *Moed Katan*, 3:11, quoted in *Chidushei R. Akiva Eiger* on *Shulchan Aruch Yoreh De'ah* 265:1; *Koreis HaBris, Posach Eliyahu* 9; *Bris Avos* 8:37 and footnote loc. cit.; *Chayim U'Brachah LeMishmeres Shalom* Letter *shin*:41.

CHAPTER SEVENTEEN
NAMING A CHILD AFTER SOMEONE WHO DIED, BUT HAS NOT YET BEEN BURIED

1) A child should not be named after someone who has died, but has not yet been buried.[1]

---

1. See *Responsa Teshuras Shai* by R. Shlomo Yehuda Tanak (1st edition), 5: "In my opinion, a child should not be named after someone who has died, but has not yet been buried." This accords with the statement in *Zohar Parshas Emor*:

    After the soul departs from the body, and the body remains without a spirit, it is forbidden to leave [the body] unburied, for it interferes with the carrying out of G-d's plans. For example, G-d may have decreed that [this soul] should be transferred to another reincarnation immediately, on the same day as the death, for its own benefit. But so long as the body remains unburied, the soul cannot come before the Holy One, nor can it enter another body as a second reincarnation. A second body is not given to a soul until the first one has been buried.

    This means that the soul of the deceased cannot be reincarnated until after the burial. See also the commentary of *Rikanti, Parshas Teitzei*:

    In order not to delay implementing G-d's decrees, He has commanded us not to keep [the body unburied] overnight. So long as [the body] remains unburied, [the soul] will not be reincarnated. This is the same as a man, who would not marry another wife before the first one is buried. Therefore, He has commanded us to bury him immediately, for perhaps he will then immediately find a suitable repose.

    As before, this implies that there is no reincarnation until after burial. Now, it is explained in several places that the soul of the deceased is reincarnated in the child who is named after the deceased. Therefore, in our case — where the deceased has not yet been buried — it cannot yet be reincarnated, and therefore the child should not be named after the deceased. See the conclusion of *Responsa Teshuras Shai*, loc. cit.

    In light of this, we must consider the case of a father who died on the day that he was to circumcise his son. The common custom is to name the child at the time of the circumcision, but it is also the custom to name him after the father, provided that he is buried before the circumcision. Now, *Yoreh De'ah* 300 states that if there are both a burial and a circumcision, the circumcision is done first. Nevertheless, in our case it would seem that the burial should be done first, for the reasons I have stated.

See above, ch. 10, paragraph 7, note 13. See also *Chayim U'Berachah LeMishmeres Shalom* (by R. Shalom Schachna Chernik), Letter *shin*: 40: "Regarding naming after the deceased, see *Responsa Teshuras Shai*, stating that a child should not be named after someone who died, but has not yet been buried, according to *Zohar* and *Rikanti*." See also *Responsa Mishneh Halachos* (by R. Menashe Klein), Vol. 4, ch. 152, who also rules that one should not give a name after someone who has not yet been buried. See also *Responsa Minchas Elazar*, Vol. 4, ch. 27, and *Darkei Chayim VeShalom*, addenda to no. 929.

Chapter Eighteen
Naming a Child According to the Calendar

1) A person should not name his son according to the year of the century in which he was born. For example: if it was the fourteenth year of the century, he should not name him "David," whose letters add up to the number fourteen.¹

2) Some have the custom to name a child according to the *parshah* of the week in which he was born. For example: in *parshas Shemos*, the child is named Moshe or Aharon; i.e., after the subject of that week's *parshah*.²

3) If a boy is born on Shabbos, some have the custom to name him Shabsi.³

4) If a child has his *bris* on Rosh HaShanah, some have the custom to name him Yitzchak.⁴

5) If a child is born on Yom Kippur, some have the custom to name him Rachamim ["mercy"].⁵

6) If a child is born on some festival, some have the custom to name him Yom Tov. If a child has his *bris* during Sukkos,

---

1. See *Sefer Chassidim* 502: "One used to call [his son] David [because of the number of the year]. The son died, because the Holy One does not desire that the years remain forever; each year must be set aside to make place for the succeeding year."
2. See *Bris Avos* 8:31, stating that this custom derives from what is written in *Tashbetz* regarding Tishah BeAv and Purim. See later, also quoted in *Sefer HaBris* p. 318, paragraph 19.
3. See *Responsa Divrei Chayim*, Vol. 2, *Even HaEzer* 134.
4. See *Leket Yosher* (customs and rulings of the author of *Terumas HaDeshen*), quoted in *Sefer HaBris*, p. 317, paragraph 19:
5. See the memorial book *Bris LaRishonim*, quoted in *Sefer HaBris*, loc. cit.

some have the custom to name him after the *Ushpiz* ["guest"] of that day.[6]

7) If a child is born during Chanukah, some have the custom to name him after the *Nasi* ["prince"] of that day. Others say that he should be named Matisyahu.[7] In some Sephardic communities, such a child is named Chanukah.

8) If a child has his *bris* on Purim, some have the custom to name him Mordechai.[8]

9) If a girl is born on Purim, some have the custom to name her Esther.[9]

10) If a child is born at the beginning of the month of Nisan, some have the custom to name him after the *Nasi* of that day,[10] or to name him after the month, "Nisan." If a child is born during Pesach, some have the custom to name him Pesach.

11) If a child has his *bris* on Tishah BeAv, some have the custom to name him Menachem; if the father, or an older son, is named Menachem, then the child is named Nechemiah.[11] Some say that all this is done only if the circumcision takes place after midday.[12]

12) If a girl is born on Tishah BeAv, some have the custom to name her Bas Tzion.[13]

---

6. See *Bris Avos* 8:39, quoted in *Sefer HaBris*, p. 318, paragraph 19.
7. See *Bris Avos* loc. cit.; see also *Bris LaRishonim*, quoted in *Sefer HaBris*, loc. cit.
8. See *Responsa Tashbetz*, Vol. 3, ch. 8, quoted in *Bris Avos*, loc. cit., and in *Sefer HaBris*, p. 317, paragraph 19; *Taamei HaMinhagim*, p. 291, note 652, in *Kuntres Acharon*.
9. See the periodical *Yeshurun*, 2nd Year (Teves 5675) p. 38, the essay by R. Yitzchak Dov HaLevy Bamberg; *Responsa Zechor Simchah* 224, quoted in *VeYikarei Shemo BeYisrael*, p. 42.
10. See *Bris Avos*, loc. cit. and *Sefer HaBris*, p. 318, paragraph 19.
11. See *Responsa Tashbetz*, loc. cit.
12. See *Koreis HaBris*, quoted in *Bris Avos*, loc. cit. and *Sefer HaBris*, loc. cit.
13. See sources cited above, in footnote 9.

CHAPTER NINETEEN
NAMING A CHILD ACCORDING TO THE CIRCUMSTANCES OF HIS BIRTH

1) If an unmarried woman gives birth to a son, some say that he should be named Zundel ["little sin"].¹ Others say that he should be named Isser ["forbidden"].²

2) If a *mamzer* is born, some say that he should be named Kidor, after the verse (*Devarim* 32:20) *Ki dor tahapuchos heima* ["for they are a generation of contradictions].³ Others disagree, saying that they may give him any name they wish.⁴

---

1. See *Bris Avos* 8:33; *Sefer HaBris*, p. 318, paragraph 22.
2. See *Zocheir HaBris* 24:17; *Sefer HaBris*, loc. cit.
3. *Taz* on *Yoreh De'ah*, *Hilchos Milah* 265:8, quoting *Maharil*.
4. *Responsa Chayim BaYad*, 70:
    Regarding what name to give him, *Maharil* (quoted by *Shach*, *Yoreh De'ah* 265, comment 8) writes, "He should be named Kidor, after the verse (*Devarim* 32:20) *Ki dor tahapuchos heima*, as we find in *Yoma* 83." But in my humble opinion, it makes no sense to give him a name as a *rasha*. Even if he is a *mamzer*, he is obligated to do all the *mitzvos*; furthermore, we are told at the end of *Horayos* that a *mamzer* who is a Torah scholar takes precedence over a *Kohen Gadol* who is an ignoramus. Thus, if this *mamzer* were a *Kohen*, he would have the privilege of reading the Torah first.
    Chinuch on *Teitzei*, no. 560, writes: "We are commanded that he should not marry any daughter of the congregation of G-d. But regarding his dwelling with them wherever they live, and to do all sorts of business with them, this is truly permitted, as with any one of the children of Israel. In fact, the Sages have said that a *mamzer* who is a Torah scholar takes precedence over an ignoramus at the Torah reading."
    This being the case, why would we penalize the *mamzer*? What sin or transgression has he committed? It is not he who sinned, but his father and mother. The *Zohar* even says that about him it was said, "Behold

3) Regarding a questionable *mamzer*, there are two opinions. Some say that he should not be given any name that is reserved for a *mamzer*, for this would constitute calling one's fellow Jew by a shameful name. Others say that he should be named Zundel, or given one of the names from the period prior to Avraham *Avinu*, to signify that the child has a questionable pedigree.[5]

4) If an orphan is born, whose father and mother are both dead — some name such a child Uri Shraga, or Schneur. This serves as memorial lamps for the souls of both his parents. Some name an orphan Yerucham, after the verse (*Hoshea* 14:4)

---

the tears of the oppressed, there is none to comfort them." Thus, since he is a Jew obligated by all the *mitzvos* of the Torah, what purpose is there in calling him by a wicked name, making a sort of prophetic statement that he will be a *rasha* (G-d forbid)?

I also suspect that this would constitute the sin of placing an obstacle before the blind, for by giving him this name we cause him to be a *rasha* and sinner. A similar thing is written in *Sefer Chassidim* 440: if one interprets a dream for a gentile, to mean that he will worship idols; or he interprets a dream for his fellow Jew, to mean that he will sin, he transgresses the sin of placing an obstacle before the blind. The same thing is written in *Sefer HaBris* — If interpreting a dream, saying that one will commit a sin, causes it to come true, and transgresses placing an obstacle before the blind, how much more so is this true regarding one who gives another person a wicked name, for certainly, that person will then continue the deeds of that *rasha* Kidor.

But besides all this, the name [Kidor] indicates [that he is a *mamzer*]; and it is written in *Sefer Chassidim* 245, 246 that one should not give names after those with wicked traits. Moreover, the rule is that we do not speak the names of *reshaim*, as written in *Yoma* 38a. It is not proper to call a *mamzer* Kidor; for then, if he turns out to be a *rasha* and sinner, people will say that the name has caused it, and thus we will be responsible for it.

On the other hand, if he turns out to be a *tzaddik* rather than a sinner — especially if he is a Torah scholar — how can he possibly bear the wicked name of Kidor? We would thus be putting him to shame in public, each time we call him by this evil name. There is no legal objection to our mentioning the fact that he is a *mamzer*; on the contrary, it is our obligation to publicize this, in fulfillment of the law of the Torah forbidding others to marry him. This, in fact, preserves his life, for *mamzerim* remain alive only so long as their status is public knowledge. But Kidor is the name of a *rasha* and sinner.

5. See *Sefer HaBris*, loc. cit.

Asher becha yerucham yasom[6] ["for through You shall the orphan be comforted"].

---

6. As we know, the *Amora* Abaye's name is an acronym of *Asher becha yerucham yasom*; because he was an orphan, he was given this name. See *Yuchsin HaShaleim*, entry on "Abaye."

CHAPTER TWENTY
SOMEONE WHOSE SON OR DAUGHTER HAS DIED (G-D FORBID)

1) If a person sees that his children fail to survive, it is a fact that their name is the cause of it. Therefore, he should be very careful about what name he gives to the next child born.[1]

2) Some say that if one of his sons dies, he should not give the next son the same name as the one who died, for this will cause misfortune.[2] Others disagree, saying that he may give the next son the same name as the brother who died.[3]

3) Some say that the next child should be given two names[4] — the name of the child who died, together with a new name; and the new name should come first.[5] People should then call him by the new name.[6]

---

1. *Sefer Chassidim* 246 and 244; quoted in *Sefer Bris Avos* 8:9.
2. See *Pischei Teshuvah*, *Yoreh De'ah* 115:5:6, quoting *Responsa Adnei Paz* 25; also quoted in *Darkei Teshuvah*, ibid:48.
3. See *Darkei Teshuvah*, loc. cit., quoting *Responsa* of *Ramatz*. The Mitteler Rebbe named his youngest daughter Sarah, after his eldest daughter, who passed away in her youth.
4. See *Ikrei Hadat*, *Yoreh De'ah*, *Hilchos Kibbud Av VaEm*, quoting "a certain chassid"; this is also quoted in *Bris Avos* 8:24.
5. The G'ra revealed this charm to his daughter, whose children died while they were young. This was done — the child who had died most recently had been named Dov Ber, and the next child to be born was named Zalman Ber. This son survived. See *Bris Avos* 8:27, quoting what the G'ra wrote in *Aliyos Eliyahu*, p. 34, footnote 51; also quoted in *Darkei Teshuvah*, loc. cit.
6. See *Bris Avos* 8:27, stating that the detail about people calling him by the new name was not instructed by the G'ra, but rather someone else, who added this on his own.

4) Some say — quoting *Yerushalmi* — that the next son to be born should be named Ben Tzion.[7]

5) Some say that the next son should be given a name that contains the Name of G-d, such as: Shmuel, Rephael, Michael, Yisrael, Yermiyah, Eliyahu, Yeshayah, and the like.[8]

6) Some have the custom that a person whose earlier children died should not give the next son any name at the *bris*. Instead, the child is called Alter ["old one"]; Only when he has grown older should his father give him his proper name.[9]

7) Some have the custom that — to protect their child from sickness — they give the name of some animal, believing that this will protect him. Thus, they give names such as Tzvi ["deer"], Ari ["lion"], etc.[10]

8) Some say that if a person's earlier children died, then when the next child is born he should sell the child to another family, or to the congregation.[11]

---

7. *Chida*, in *Shem HaGedolim*, section 2, later additions, paragraph 1; quoted in *Bris Avos* 8:25; *Sefer HaBris*, p. 317, paragraph 18; *Taamei HaMinhagim*, p. 570.
8. See *Yosef Ometz, Hilchos Gidul Banim*; quoted in *Bris Avos* 8:26. See also ch.7, above.
9. See *Bris Avos* 8:25:
   The correct procedure is to record the name in some sort of code, so that others will be unaware of the correct name until the child grows older. But if he does not do this, and he gives the child his proper name at the *bris*, then even adding the name Alter will not help at all..
   See also *Taamei HaMinhagim* 929, quoting *Midbar Kedeimos*, stating that Noach's father did not give him his proper name until he grew older.
10. See *Bris Avos* 8:23, quoting *Shem HaGedolim* by *Chida*, stating that this is the custom in Italy.
11. *Sefer Chassidim* 245; see also the comment of *Mekor Chesed* loc. cit.; *Responsa Chasam Sofer, Choshen Mishpat* 111.

CHAPTER TWENTY-ONE
GIVING TWO CHILDREN THE SAME NAME

1) Some say that one should not give two of his children the same name — regardless of whether both are living (because of the evil eye), or if the first one has died (because this name has caused misfortune).[1]

2) Others disagree, saying that a person may give two of his children the same name.[2]

---

1. See *Responsa Adnei Paz* 25 and 34; quoted in *Pischei Teshuvah, Yoreh De'ah* 116:106 and *Darkei Teshuvah* loc. cit., paragraph 48. See also *Pardes Yosef* on the Torah (by R. Yosef Partzanavski), *Bereishis* 4:25; similarly, op cit., *Shemos Parshas Yisro* 18:3.

    See *Pardes Yosef* loc. cit., who proves it from Scripture, "For G-d has presented me with other seed in place of Hevel":
    > This appears difficult to understand — if her primary purpose was to memorialize her son Hevel who was dead, why did she not give him the same name, Hevel, after his deceased brother? This therefore indicates that one should not give the same name to two children.

    See *Siach Sarfei Kodesh*, Vol. 5, p. 100, paragraph 28:
    > I asked him (i.e., the Rebbe of Sochatchov) whether the child just born should be named after the child who had died, as stated in various *seforim* quoting the *G'ra*. But he would not consent to this, but gave no reason for it.

2. See the above citations, quoting *Responsa Ramatz, Yoreh De'ah* 88. See also *Responsa Shoel U'Meishiv* (2nd edition), Vol. 3, ch. 15; *Responsa Toras Nesanel* 20; *Neta Sorek, Yoreh De'ah* 50; comment of *Mekor Chesed* on *Sefer Chassidim*, loc. cit. See also *Tikkunei Zohar Chadash*, p. 44. Explicit proof is offered from Scripture (*I Divrei HaYamim* 6:8), "... and Yivchar and Elishama and Eliphelet..."; in verse 8 it says, "...and Elishama and Elyada and Eliphelet make nine. *Rashi*, loc. cit. comments that in *II Shmuel* 2:5, Eliphelet is listed only once, and there are a total of seven whereas here the total is nine. The reason is that his son Eliphelet had died, and later another son was born whose name was also Eliphelet, and he is the one listed later.. Another proof is cited from *Rashi* on *Kesuvos* 89b, on the passage "Mar Kashisha and Mar Yenuka"; *Rashi* comments: "Rav Chisda had two sons, and both had the same name, but [to distinguish them] the elder was known as Mar Kashisha ["the elder"] and the younger was known as Mar Yenuka ["the younger"]. (See also *Tosafos* on *Bava Basra* 7b, on the passage "Mar Yenuka."

Chapter Twenty-Two
Special Objections Regarding Names

1) Some say that a person should not name three sons Avraham, Yitzchak, and Yaakov.¹ Others say that this is only if they are given consecutively, one after the other.² Commonly, people are not particular about this.³

2) It is written in the *Testament of R. Yehudah HaChassid* that none of his descendants should name his son Yehudah or Shmuel. Some comment that this instruction was only for his own family, or for his own contemporaries.⁴

3) It is written in various *seforim* that a person should not name his son Moshe or Shmuel.⁵

---

1. See *Chochmas HaNefesh*, quoted in *Bris Avos* 8:17:6. See also *Sefer HaBris*, p. 317. See additional warnings in the *Testament of R. Yehudah HaChassid*, ch. 2, and in *Mekor Chesed*, loc. cit.
2. See *Sefer HaBris*, loc. cit., paragraph 17, who so interprets the text of *Chochmas HaNefesh*.
3. Because it is likely that the author wrote this only for his own family, or for his own contemporaries. See *Bris Avos*, loc. cit., paragraph 17.
4. See *Bris Avos* 8:12; *Responsa Noda BiYehudah* (2nd edition), *Even HaEzer* 79; *Responsa Divrei Chayim, Even HaEzer* 8. See also *Likkutei Halachos* on the *Testament of R. Yehudah HaChassid*, and *Mekor Chesed* on the *Testament of R. Yehudah HaChassid*, 51:69.
5. See *Chochmas HaNefesh*, loc. cit., quoted ibid. See *Sefer HaBris*, p. 314. *Bris Avos* 46 questions whether the objection of *Chochmas HaNefesh* refers to naming two sons Moshe and Shmuel (i.e., one Moshe and the other Shmuel); or whether he means combining the two names Moshe Shmuel for one son; or whether he means naming three sons Avraham, Moshe, and Shmuel.

Chapter Twenty-Three
Non-Jewish Names

1) It is forbidden to call oneself, or one's child, by a non-Jewish name.[1]

---

1. This is because of the prohibition of "You shall not follow their statutes"; see *Responsa Maharam Schick*, *Yoreh De'ah* 169, quoted in *Darkei Teshuvah* 178: 14; *Pischei Teshuvah*, Vol. 2, ch. 198; *Encyclopedia Talmudica*, Vol. 17, entry on *Chukos HaGoyim*, paragraph 5. See *Sedei Chemed, Kuntres HaKlalim*, letter *reish*, paragraph 41; ibid., letter *zayin*; see also *Taamei HaMinhagim, Likkutim*, — *al titosh Toras imecha*, footnote on p. 555, quoting various *seforim* on this subject; see also *Responsa Rashdam*, *Yoreh De'ah* 199. See *Responsa Maharsham*, Vol. 6, ch. 10:
   > Regarding the custom nowadays that people call themselves by non-Jewish names, this is a dangerous thing, for it is one of the things that delay the redemption. The Sages in *Bamidbar Rabbah* 20:22 (see also *Maharal, Gevuros HaShem* 43) counted the fact that they did not change their names, among the merits for which the Jews in Egypt were redeemed; this is [the merit] that supported our ancestors...

   It is similarly stated in *seforim*, quoting *Yalkut HaGershuni*, that this is why the king of Egypt commanded Yocheved and Miriam to change their names to Shifra and Puah — to deprive them of the merit of "they did not change their names."

   See also *Maayanah Shel Torah*, commenting on *Shemos* 1:15, "And the king of Egypt said to the Hebrew midwives, one of whose names was...," quoting R. Tzvi Elimelech of Dinov, who interprets this verse as follows:
   > Pharaoh knew that so long as the midwives were called by their Jewish names Yocheved and Miriam, he would be unable to persuade them to obey the cruel decree of killing the Jewish children. Therefore, he first commanded them to change their names to Shifra and Puah; he thought that once they were called by their Egyptian names, this would have a psychological effect upon them. It would change their essential character and natures to such an extent that they would now be capable of murdering Jewish children. Only then did he give them the second commandment, "but if it be a boy, you shall kill him."

2) Some say that this is only if one calls himself by a specifically gentile name. But if he merely translates his Jewish name to its equivalent in another language, it is permitted.²

3) Others find reason to permit calling oneself by a non-Jewish name.³

4) People who already have non-Jewish names,, and later were given Jewish names, are permitted to continue using their non-Jewish names when doing business with people who know them only by their non-Jewish names.⁴

---

2. See *Responsa Tzofnas Paneiach* 275, quoted in *Encyclopedia Talmudica*, loc. cit. See also *Yosef Ometz*, p. 362: "it is because of our bitter exile that the uncircumcised gentiles change our holy names to other names against our will." Thus we may understand why many great rabbis of Israel had foreign names; for example: R. Yehudah HaLevy was called in Arabic Abu Al Chasan; *Rambam* was called in Arabic Abu Amran Mussa; *Ramban* was called in Castillian Magister Bonstruk de Porta; and there are many more examples. See *Responsa Tzofnas Paneiach*, ibid.; see *Taamei HaMinhagim*, footnote on p. 555.

3. See *Responsa Ein Yehudah* (by R. Eliezer Yehudah Rabinowitz), "Miscellaneous," ch. 12. He cites proof from the famous *Aggadah* regarding Alexander the Great — the Jews named their sons born in that year after him (*Yoma* 87; Josephus; *Raavad* in *Sefer HaKabbalah* 32:2). He also cites proof from Onkelus the Convert — his Greek name was Akilas, which the Jews mispronounced as Onkelus. See also *Gittin* 12b, stating that the majority of Jews in the Diaspora have names resembling those of the idolaters; see the comments of R. Tzvi Hirsh Chayus on *Tosafos*, loc. cit., passage beginning "Bati," stating that the name he had had while still a gentile remained with him after he converted. See also *Zohar Chadash* on *Rus* 9a; *Nachalas Tzvi* 167.

4. *Responsa Maharashdam, Yoreh De'ah* 199, regarding people who had come from Portugal, because they feared that it would seem like they were still behaving like gentiles, and did not believe in G-d or His Torah.

Since we are on the subject, it is worthwhile to cite *Darkei Moshe*, revised, biography of *Maharam Schick*, (compiled by R. Chananya Yom Tov Lipa Braun), 1:

> Our master, the *gaon Maharam Schick* received the tradition from his parents regarding the origin of their family name Schick: when the Imperial decree was issued in Austria that every Jewish family must have a surname, the first one to have the family name Schick was concerned about the decree of the early Sages forbidding one to call himself by a non-Jewish name. Therefore, he chose the name Schick, which is an acronym for *Shem Yisrael Kodesh* ["the name of Israel is holy"]. This is evidenced by the fact that originally the name Schick was written with a double apostrophe, to signify that it was an acronym.

I will also mention what is cited in *Sefas Emes*, commenting on the verse, "And these are the names of those coming to Egypt" — several early and late commentators have asked about the word "coming," in the present tense; it ought to have said, "who *came* to Egypt," in the past tense. *Sefas Emes* explains that this refers to those who come to Egypt in every generation; i.e., whenever the Jews are afflicted in each succeeding exile, these "names" of the Tribes of Israel come to protect them with their merits, so that they will not assimilate among the gentiles.

CHAPTER TWENTY-FOUR
NAMES PREDATING AVRAHAM *AVINU*

1) Some say that one should give his child only names mentioned in the Torah from Avraham *Avinu* and later. But we do not call ourselves by names mentioned in the Torah before Avraham *Avinu*.[1]

2) Some limit the above specifically to naming one's child after a person mentioned in the Torah before Avraham *Avinu* — this should not be done. For example, one should not name his son Noach specifically after the Noach mentioned in the Torah. But, if he names his son Noach for some other reason, or for no particular reason, it is permitted.[2]

3) Others say that we need not be particular about this, and that one is permitted to give his child even names mentioned in the Torah before Avraham *Avinu*.[3]

---

1. See *Responsa Mabit*, Vol. 1, ch. 276, quoted in *Sefer HaBris*, p. 308; *Shem HaGedolim* by *Chida*; *Otzar Dinin U'Minhagim*, p. 248.
2. See *Bris Avos* 8:34, citing proof from Moshe *Rabbeinu*, who had no compunction about naming his son Eliezer, because he did not name him after Eliezer the slave of Avraham, but for a different reason.
3. *Birkei Yosef, Yoreh De'ah* 265:6 concludes that people are generally not particular about this. See *K'nesses HaGedolah, Yoreh De'ah* 265:8, questioning the opinion of *Mabit*, who forbids giving names that predate Avraham *Avinu*. See also *Responsa Teshuvah MeAhavah*, Vol. 1, ch. 35, quoted in *Pischei Teshuvah, Yoreh De'ah* 265:6; *Responsa Tesuvos VeHanhagos* 605. Concerning this subject in general, see *Responsa Rashba*, Vol. 4., ch. 30.

CHAPTER TWENTY-FIVE
"MAY THE NAME OF *RESHAIM* DECAY"

1) It is forbidden to give one's child the same name as a *rasha*.[1] Some add that this prohibition is not only upon the father; even if he has already given his son the name of a *rasha* (because he did not know it was forbidden), the public is forbidden to call him by this name. They should substitute a nickname, and call him by this nickname.[2] Others say that this

---

1. This follows the *Gemara, Yoma* 38b: "What is meant by 'May the Name of *Reshaim* Decay?' R. Eliezer says, 'Let mold grow upon their names, for we do not call ourselves by their names.'" See the commentary of R. Chananel, who says that if one calls his son by the name of a *rasha*, he will not succeed in life, for the name of a *rasha* serves as a curse upon the child's life. See also *Midrash Rabbah, Bereishis* 49:1:
   > Said R. Shmuel bar Nachman: The names of *reshaim* are leather garments — the more they are worn, the longer they last; but when they are no longer worn, they rot. In a similar vein: have you ever heard of someone naming his son Pharaoh, Sisera, or Sancherev? Rather, they are named Avraham, Yitzchak, Yaakov, Reuven, Shimon..."

   See also *Midrash Shmuel*, ch. 1; *Sefer Chassidim* section 1000:
   > Why did Chanoch and Lemech live such short lives? Because [Chanoch] bore the name of Chanoch the son of Kayin, and Lemech bore the same name as Lemech the son of Mesushael. As for Kayin and his descendants, "May the name of *reshaim* decay!"

   See also *Chidushei Aggados Maharsha, Taanis* 28a: "...and it is forbidden to give someone the name of a *rasha*." See also *Otzar Dinim U'Minhagim*, p. 422; *Responsa Torosh VeYitzhar* 108.
2. See the essay by R. Simchah Kahn, "Calling one's son Avshalom," printed in his book, *Laws of Intermarriage and Conversion*.

is only a precaution taken by those who are extra pious, but it is not actually forbidden.³

2) If there is a *tzaddik* whose name is the same as that of the *rasha*, then one may give his child this name.⁴ Some say that it is better to add a name, and to call the child by both names.⁵ Others are more strict, saying that if it is well known that this is the name of a *rasha* — and the *tzaddik* with the same name is obscure — one should not give his child this name.⁶

3) This prohibition applies only to one who was completely wicked. But an individual sin does not make one a *rasha* whose name may not be used.⁷

4) If one wishes to name his child after someone who desecrated the Shabbos, then some say that if it is a common name such as Avraham, Yaakov, Moshe, or Aharon, one need not worry about it, and may give the child his name. But, it is better to add an additional name.⁸

5) If a *rasha* did *teshuvah*, one may give a child his name.⁹

6) Some say that this prohibition involves only someone who was a *rasha* from the beginning. But if one became a *rasha* [later in life], it is not forbidden to use his name.¹⁰

7) Some say that we may use the names of *reshaim* mentioned in the Torah¹¹; or, names given by the Holy One.¹²

---

3. The reason is that *Poskim* did not codify the rule that we do not call ourselves by their names. See *Shaar HaMelech* discussing *Rambam's* Introduction, and *Ateres Chachamim*, essay by R. Nasan Nata Zuber.
4. *Tosafos, Yoma*, loc. cit., on the passage *delo*; *Tosafos, Shabbos* 12b; *Responsa* of *Rama* 41; *Sdei Chemed, Kelalim*, Letter *zayin* 7; *Responsa Teshuvos VeHanhagos* 606.
5. Ibid.
6. See *Sefer HaMakneh, Kesubos* 104b, discussing opinion of *Rabbeinu Tam*.
7. *Piskei Tosafos, Sotah* 20.
8. See *Responsa Teshuvos VeHanhagos* op. cit.
9. *Tosafos Yeshanim* and *Ritva, Yoma*, loc. cit. ask how the name Yishmael is found among *tzaddikim*; the answer is that Yishmael did *teshuvah*. See *Responsa Min HaShamayim* 190 and *Responsa Mevaser Tov*, discussing why we find the name Yishmael, but not the name Esav.
10. *Responsa Divrei Yaakov; Maharsham, Yoma* loc. cit.

8) Some say that we may call someone by a name of *reshaim* that is not a proper name.[13]

9) Some say that this is only forbidden if the name itself reveals that the person was a *rasha*.[14]

10) Some say that a person named Avshalom should change his name to Avishalom or to Av-Shalom (making it two names); one does not thus contravene the honor due to his father by altering the name his father gave him as a child.[15]

11) One should not name his son after someone who was excommunicated.[16] Some say that this is only if that person died while under the ban; but, if he lived under the ban for a period of time, and then the ban was rescinded, one may name a child after him.[17] Others are more strict, saying that if he had remained excommunicated for thirty days, it can never be rescinded, and one may not name a child after him.[18]

12) Several *mohalim* inquired of the rabbinic authorities in *Eretz Yisrael* what to do in a case where someone wishes to give his son the name of a *rasha*, "Nimrod." The reply was that there are two options: i) the *mohel* should leave immediately after the circumcision, before the name is given; ii) the *mohel* should try to persuade the father to give the son two names — one a

---

11. *Yosef Ometz* by *Chida*, quoted in *Sdei Chemed*, *Kelalim*, Letter *reish*, 41; *Maharsham*, loc. cit.
12. *Tosafos Yeshanim* loc. cit., explaining that we find *tzaddikim* named Yishmael because the Holy One Himself gave this name.
13. See *Shoshanim LeDavid*, *Yoma* 3:11; *Midrash Eliyahu*, explaining that the prophet Michah was named Michah because in *Sanhedrin* 101b it is stated that Nevot and Michah were not the *rasha's* proper names.
14. *Penei Yehoshua*, *Kesubos* 104b.
15. R. Moshe Tendler, quoting his father-in-law, R. Moshe Feinstein; printed in *Nisuei Taaruvos VeGeirus*.
16. *Sefer Chassidim* 1102.
17. See *Bris Avos* 8:41, who so interprets *Sefer Chassidim*.
18. See *Bris Avos*, loc. cit.

secular name, and the other a holy name; the name of the *rasha* should be the secular name.[19]

---

19. See R. BenTzion Kaganov, *History of Jewish Names*, p. 82. We will also cite *Chida* in *Devash LeFi*, letter *shin*, note 20:

> One's name is his soul, and thus, the Sages speculate about the name of Moshiach, for that is his soul. The Sages also say that a foe is unable to mention the name of his adversary, but a friend mentions the name of his loved one many repeatedly. This is how I interpret the verse, "Is Ephraim not My beloved son, is he not a playful child?": [G-d is saying]: "I love him as one loves a baby, and therefore, 'whenever I speak of him' — though I am already on the subject and have no need to mention his name — I nevertheless mention it repeatedly, because of My great love; 'Therefore My inner parts stir for him, I will surely have compassion on him' — this is a great and manifold love. This accords with what we have said before: since the name is the soul, the name gives a hint of the soul's attachment on High. Based on this principle, I interpret the saying of the Sages, that the Holy One instructed the Angels to name [His creatures], but they did not know how; then, he instructed Adam to do so, and he gave the names. Now this seems strange — how much wisdom is involved in combining a few letters to form a name? But, since the name reveals a hint of the source of the soul in the supernal realms, the ministering Angels did not know, but Adam did know how each created being was attached to the source of holiness in its own unique fashion, and he named it accordingly.

CHAPTER TWENTY-SIX
NAMING AN ADOPTED CHILD

1) When a adopting a child who was born to gentiles, he is circumcised; but he is not given a Jewish name until he is a bit older and can undergo the immersion, i.e., at about two years of age. Then, he is immersed in the presence of a *beis din*, and given a Jewish name.[1]

2) If the foster parents are embarrassed by the fact that no name is given at the *bris*, then they may give him a name then. But the words "in Israel" should be omitted; i.e., the blessing should be, "...and let his name be called ... *ben* ...," not "...and let his name be called in Israel..."[2]

3) If the adopted child is a girl, she should not be given a name until she is a bit older and can undergo the immersion. She should be named immediately after the immersion, without waiting for a day when the Torah is read — it is better to do it at the time of immersion.[3]

4) The rules concerning a child adopted from Jewish parents: whose name does he use when signing a document, or when called up to the Torah — the name of his biological father, or that of his foster father? There are different opinions regarding such cases.

---

1. See *Responsa Igros Moshe, Yoreh De'ah*, ch. 161.
2. Ibid. See also *Koreis HaBris*, et. al., who rule that if a Jewish woman conceives a child by a gentile, the child is given a name, but the words "in Israel" are omitted.
3. *Igros Moshe*, loc. cit.

Some say that when adopting a child [from gentiles], he should not be named at the *bris*, but rather after the immersion; Others disagree, saying that such a child should be named at the *bris*; they should not say "...*ben* Avraham *Avinu*" as is done with other converts, but instead the child is named as the son of the foster father.[4]

If one who was adopted signs his name as the son of his foster father, the document remains valid. Similarly, if the foster father describes the adopted son as his own son, it is valid.[5]

Some say that when he is called up to the Torah, he should be called by the name of his foster father.[6] Others say that he

---

4. Ibid.
5. See *Rama, Choshen Mispat*, end of 42; *Responsa Rashba*, Vol. 4, ch. 197. See also *Midrash Rabbah, Parshas Tisa* 46:
>The Holy One said to [the Jews]: You have set aside your forefathers Avraham, Yitzchak, and Yaakov, and you call Me your father. They replied to him, It is You whom we recognize as our father. The situation may be likened to an orphan girl who was raised by her guardian. He was a good and trustworthy man, who raised her and cared for her properly. When he sought to marry her off, the stenographer came to write a *kesubah*, he asked her, "What is your name?" She replied, "[My name is] ..." He then asked, "And what is your father's name?" At first, she was silent, so her guardian said to her, "Why are you silent?" She replied, "Because I know no other father but you." This implies that the foster father is called the father, and not the one who begat her.

>We also note the famous case of the *Amora* Abaye: his father died while his mother was pregnant with him, and his mother died during childbirth. His paternal uncle Rabbah bar Nachmani adopted him, and named him Abaye, which is an acronym for of *Asher becha yerucham yasom*; nevertheless, we find that the Sages called him Nachmani (*Shabbos* 33a; 74a; et. al.). He also called his aunt who raised him by the name Eim ["mother"], and he gave her the honor due to one's mother.

6. See *Responsa Chasam Sofer, Even HaEzer* 76, who rules that a stepson should be called up to the Torah by the name of the one who raises him.
Regarding the case where the biological father is a *Kohen* and the foster father is a *Levi*, R Mordechai HaKohen rules in *Halachos VeHalichos*:
>It seems to me that the rule of calling him up to the Torah by his foster father's name applies only to cases where the natural father is unknown to the adopted child as well as to all others, and everyone assumes him to be the foster father's child. Only in such cases is it possible — and proper — to call him up to the Torah by the foster father's name, to avoid public embarrassment to the son.

should be called by the name of his biological father.[7] A third opinion is that he is called by the name of the foster father together with the biological father.[8]

Others disagree with all the above; they hold that an adopted child is called by the name of the foster father only if this foster father has no children of his own.[9] But if the foster father has children, then there are two opinions: some say that even so, it is preferable to call the child by the name of the foster father;[10] others say that in such a case he should not be called by the name of the foster father.[11]

5) Even if the foster father has children of his own, if the adopted child is a girl, he may call her his daughter.[12]

6) If the foster father has a son of his own with the same name as the adopted child, then all authorities agree that he must not call the adopted child his son.[13]

7) Some say that if the adopted child has living parents, it is preferable that he refrain from calling the foster parent "father."[14]

---

7. See *Responsa MiMa'amakim*, Vol. 3, ch. 11. See *Responsa Minchas Yitzchak*, Vol. 4, ch 49.
8. See essay by R. Eliyahu Katz in *HaDarom*, 10 Elul 5716, pp. 32-74.
9. See *Responsa Chasam Sofer, Even HaEzer*, Vol. 1, ch. 66; *Responsa Tzitz Eliezer*; *Responsa Lev Aryeh* 26; *Responsa She'elas Yavetz* 165; *Responsa Tzir Yaakov* 33.
10. See *Urim VeTumim* on *Choshen Mishpat* 42 and *Nesivas HaMispat*, loc. cit.; *Responsa Tzitz Eliezer* op. cit.
11. *Knesses HaGedolah*, *Yavetz*, and *Chasam Sofer* hold this opinion; See *Responsa Tzitz Eliezer*, op. cit.
12. See *Responsa Tzitz Eliezer*, op. cit., who states that even according to the opinions of *Knesses HaGedolah*, et. al., this is a good thing to do. But, if the foster father has daughters of his own, *Knesses HaGedolah* rules that he should not call her his daughter.
13. See *Urim VeTumim*, end of 42; *Responsa Tzitz Eliezer*, op. cit.
14. See *Responsa Tzitz Eliezer*, op. cit.; *Responsa Yavetz*, Vol. 1, ch. 165, regarding one who utters a vow to forbid himself to derive any benefit from his father, without specifying which father; he questions whether this should be taken to mean the natural father, or the foster father, and rules that it is necessary to adopt the stringencies of both.

CHAPTER TWENTY-SEVEN
NAMING A CHILD WHO DIED

1) If a child dies before reaching the age of eight days, he is circumcised before burial, and given a name.[1] Some have the custom to circumcise the deceased child before burial without giving him a name.[2]

2) Similarly, a baby girl who died shortly after birth is given a name.[3]

3) If the child was buried without being given a name, he is given a name after the burial.[4]

4) If a pregnant woman dies before giving birth, the fetus is given a name.[5]

---

1. The purpose of this is as a sign that Heaven should take pity upon him, and that he will be resurrected at the resurrection of the dead. See *Shulchan Aruch, Yoreh De'ah* 263:5, citing *Rosh* on *Moed Katan* no. 88:
    > Rav Nachshon says: A child who is born, and survives two days, or three or four, and then dies, our custom here is to circumcise him at the grave and to give him a name so that when Heaven has mercy and there is a resurrection of the dead, this child will be known, and his father will know who he is.

    Korban Nesanel, loc. cit. 20:
    > By giving him a name, the child will be known; his father will be aware that he once had a son named ..., and thus the father will know him. The son will thus also know his father.
2. See *Nechmad LeMareh*, Vol. 1, p. 128.
3. See *Sdei Chemed*, section on mourning, ch. 202. See also *Responsa Heishiv Moshe* 13: "The reason that people are not careful to do this is that they are unaware [that it should be done]."
4. See *Responsa Meir Nesivim* 47.
5. See *Responsa Heishiv Moshe, Orach Chayim* 13:
    > The custom in some communities is that if a pregnant woman dies, they pronounce a decree that she must expel the fetus. If it is not expelled,

the suspicion is that she fears the child will not be given a name. Therefore, three righteous men should join together as a *beis din* and approach her, saying, "... and perhaps you are afraid that the child will not be given a name; therefore, we, the *beis din* assure you that the child will be given a name, be it female or male ... and because of the giving of this name, the child will merit to rise up at the resurrection of our people." This should be recited three times in the Holy Tongue, and three times in the vernacular.

Chapter Twenty-Eight
Changing a Name

1) If a patient is sick with a serious illness, his or her name is changed.[1]

2) Some say that a name cannot be changed by ordinary people, but only by someone of special qualities.[2] But this is only to change the first and principle name. But if a name is merely being added, anyone can do it.[3]

3) When changing a man's name, the usual custom is to name him Chayim, Shalom, Rephael, Azriel, and the like; this serves as an auspicious omen that he will be recover from his illness.[4]

4) When changing a woman's name, some say that the name should not be changed to Rachel, Bas Sheva, Tamar, or

---

1. See *Rosh HaShanah* 16b; *Taanis* 15a; *Bava Kama* 125b: "Four things cause a decree of judgment against a person to be torn up; the are: charity, prayer, changing one's name, and changing one's conduct." Therefore, is someone falls sick with a serious illness, and it has been decreed in Heaven that he is to die (G-d forbid), his name is changed. Now, just as his name has been changed, his decree of judgment is changed.
2. See *Rachamei HaAv*, quoted in *Taamei HaMinhagim*, p. 105:
   G-d forbid that the name of a sick person be changed, except by someone whose every act is done by the spirit of prophecy. The name he was given after birth is certainly almost always by Divine inspiration, and it accords with his name as it is on High; it remains the person's life-force all his days. Thus, by changing his name, we may actually sever his life-force.
3. He must be careful when reciting the prayer not to remove the original name, but only to add the additional name (*Segulas Yisrael*).
4. *Otzar Dinin U'Minhagim*, p. 248.

Leah; instead, the name should be changed to Chanah, Sarah, or Yocheved.[5]

5) Some have the custom when changing a patient's name to open a *Chumash*; the patient is then given the first name of our ancestors that appears on the right hand side of the volume.[6] But if the name that appears is the name of a *rasha*, the patient is not given this name.[7] Others say that it is not proper to open a *Chumash* as a means of casting lots.[8]

6) When changing a name, the added name becomes the first name. However, if he does not recover from the illness, then, when his sons are called up to the Torah, the original name should be mentioned before the added name.[9]

7) When changing a patient's name, some say that it should be done in the patient's presence, and with a *minyan*, after reciting several chapters of the Psalms and praying for the patient.[10] Others say that the name should be changed when one of the relatives is called up to the Torah in *shul*; he takes hold of the Torah scroll, a *mi shebeirach* is recited, and then the name is changed.[11]

8) Some have the additional custom of changing the name of the patient's parents by selling a sick child to a different family, or to the entire congregation. This will save the patient

---

5. See *Devash LeFi* (by *Chida*), letter *shin*, note 14.
6. *Sefer Chassidim* 244, parenthetical clause.
7. *Responsa Mahari MiBruno* 101: it once happened that they searched the Scriptures for a name to give to a sick person; they came upon the name of a *rasha*, and *Mahari* objected to giving the patient such a name.
8. See *Chidushei Rambam* in *Kovetz Teshuvos HaRambam VeIgrosav*, Vol. 1, 52:74: *Rambam* wrote in Arabic that it is not proper to open a *Chumash* as a means of casting lots, the way the Gentiles do it. However, a communal official who did do this is not to be dismissed from his position, nor is he subject to a flogging for it.
9. *Responsa Minchas Elazar*, Vol. 4, ch. 27; *Darkei Chayim VeShalom*, addenda to ch. 929.
10. See *Sefer HaMaamarim 5709*, p. 40, regarding the Alter Rebbe's son, whose name was changed from Avraham to Chayim Avraham at home, not in *shul*.
11. *Likkutei Sichos*, Vol. 17, p. 474.

from the Divine decree that "the son of ... is to die." From this day forth, he is no longer the son of ..., but the son of someone else.[12]

9) A sinner who returns and does *teshuvah* should have his name changed.[13]

10) If someone has been married to his wife for ten years, and she has failed to produce a child, some say that her name should be changed, and that this will help her to conceive.[14]

---

12. See *Sefer Chassidim* 245:
    If one person has a son who is dying, another person should come to the parents and say to them: "Mr. and Mrs. ..., here is a *shekel* (or, here is a loaf of bread, or meat, or wine). I hereby redeem your son; let him become my son, so that he may live.
    There are several examples of names that indicate the above practice. One is the name Meshulam ["paid-for"], indicating that the child was purchased, and the sum owed has been paid. Some see an indication of this in the Talmudic names Tachlifa and Chalafta; these names indicate that the child has been exchanged for money in a sale.
13. *Rambam, Hilchos Teshuvah* 2:4,
    A characteristic of *teshuvah* is that the repentant person constantly implores G-d, with tears and supplication; he gives as much charity as he can afford, and keeps very far away from the sins he committed. He changes his name, as if to say, "I am someone else, not the person who did those deeds."
    Lechem Mishneh comments on this that according to the Talmud, any one of these is sufficient; i.e., if a person does *teshuvah* in his heart, and gives charity, even though he has not yet done any good deed, it is sufficient, and his evil judgment is torn up. Similarly, if he changes his name, even though he has not yet done any good deed, it is sufficient, for his intentions are good.
14. *Responsa Teshuvos VeHanhagos* 790.

CHAPTER TWENTY-NINE
MENTIONING THE PATIENT'S NAME, AND THAT OF HIS MOTHER, WHEN PRAYING FOR A SICK PERSON

1) If one prays for mercy on behalf of his fellow Jew, he need not mention the patient's name.[1] But if he wishes, he may do so.[2] Some say that without question one must mention the patient's name.[3] Others make a distinction: in the patient's presence, it is not necessary to mention his name; in the patient's absence, it is necessary to mention his name.[4]

2) When praying for a sick person (and reciting the *mi shebeirach*) the patient's name is mentioned together with that

---

1. *Berachos* 34a: "R. Yaakov said, quoting R. Chisda: Whoever prays for mercy on behalf of his fellow Jew, need not mention the name (of the patient: *Rashi*), as it is written, 'O G-d, please heal her, I implore You,' without mentioning Miriam's name." R. Yaakov Emden comments that perhaps the reason is that the name is known in Heaven; *Iyun Yaakov* comments that perhaps the name is what caused the illness; indeed, that is why it is customary to change the patient's name. But *Maris Ayin* (by *Chida*) questions *Iyun Yaakov's* reasoning; if that were the reason. it would not say "it is *not necessary* to mention the name," but rather "the name *should not* be mentioned."
2. See *Pri Chadash, Orach Chayim* 119, who infers from the Talmudic text "it is not necessary" that if he wishes to mention it, he may do so.
3. See *Zohar, Parshas Vayishlach*, p. 169a, on the verse, "Save me, I implore You, from the hand of my brother, the hand of Esav." This implies that one who prays must state all details of his request.
4. See *Magen Avraham* 119:1, who quotes this distinction in the name of *Maharil*. But see *Nefesh Chayah Shem*, who questions this distinction, based on an incident involving R. Chanina ben Dosa in *Taanis* 25a.

of his mother. The father's name is not mentioned.[5] The custom of some Ashkenazic communities is the mention the father's name when praying for the sick.[6]

---

5. See *Sefer Chassidim* 237:
> If one sees in a dream a gentile who has died, and the gentile instructs him to follow him, he should go to his grave and say to him that he imposes an oath upon him, insisting that he will not follow him, "I, ... ben ... [in the feminine form] do not wish to follow you, for I wish to live many more years."

Zohar, Parshas Lech Lecha 84a, on *Tehillim* 86:16: "And help the son of your maidservant"; [*Zohar* comments]: "Was he not the son of Yishai, that he had to mention his mother's name but not that of his father? But we have established the principle that when a person comes to receive something from on High, he must mention what is certain; for this reason he mentioned his mother and not his father."

Zohar, Shemos 17b: "Rabbi Yitzchak said to him: Balak was a great sorcerer; the practice of sorcerers is to use things about which there is no doubt; thus, a person's father's name is never mentioned — only the mother's name, about which there is no doubt. See also *Zohar, Parshas Yisro* 69b on the verse "...and her two sons"; [*Zohar* comments]: "R. Chiya said: were they only *her* sons and not Moshe's sons? ... R. Yosse said: though it is true that they were Moshe's sons, it is *certain* that they were her sons."

Responsa Gevul Yehudah 2 analyzes the subject: when dealing with matters of Torah law, the law was not given to Angels, and so the paternal lineage is judged according to the majority; but regarding things that are in the Heavenly realm, this is not applicable, for the real truth is revealed there. Therefore: since it is inevitable that among all the sick people for whom prayers are offered there will be one who is wrongly assumed to be the son of a certain father, the person who mentions this name in prayer will be classified among those who speak falsely before the Holy One. To avoid this, it is better to mention all patients by their mothers' names only. This is in regard to private prayer. But in public prayers for the sick another reason may be offered. There are people whose fathers are unknown. When praying for them, the name of the maternal grandfather cannot be used, for the correct name is required at prayer (unlike calling up to the Torah, where a mere hint is sufficient). If such a fictitious name for the father were to be used, it would constitute speaking falsely before the Holy One. Therefore, there would be no choice other than to treat this patient differently from others, by mentioning his mother's name. This would be an enormous public humiliation to him; to avoid embarrassing such people, the practice was adopted to mention all sick people by their mothers' names when praying.

Responsa Kisvei Eish, Vol. 1, ch. 6 writes:
> I recorded the names of the benefactors who contributed to the printing of the *sefer*, with their names and their mothers' names. Someone raised the objection that family trees are organized by paternal descent, not maternal descent; furthermore, people are called up to the Torah with

3) When someone writes a petition (*kvittel*) requesting a *tzaddik* to pray for him, he writes his name, even if the *tzaddik* knows him well;[7] he also writes his mother's name.[8]

4) When reciting the *mi shabeirach* for a woman who has given birth, the woman's name is mentioned together with her mother's name.[9] Some do it differently, mentioning her name and her father's name.[10]

5) When reciting the *E-l malei rachamim* prayer for a deceased person, and in the *yehi ratzon* prayer after studying Torah for his soul, the name of the deceased is mentioned together with his father's name.[11] Some do it differently, mentioning the deceased's name and that of his mother.[12]

---

the father's name, and so they should be recorded in a *sefer*. But my opinion is the contrary. All *tzaddikim* who receive petitions to pray for people have established the custom to write in the *kvittel* ... *ben* ... in the feminine form; this is also done in the *yehi ratzon* after studying *Mishnayos* for a deceased person. In matters of law, we follow the majority case, and do not harbor suspicions that perhaps this is not the person's father. But when praying for a sick person or studying Torah for a deceased person, we must mention a name about which there is absolute certainty, beyond any doubt...

See *Midrash Rabbah* quoted by *Rashi* on *Toldos* (27:29), "...and the sons of your mother shall bow down to you"; *Rashi* explains: Yaakov said to Yehudah, "the sons of your father," for he had sons from several wives; but here [Yitzchak] married only one wife, and so he said, "the sons of your mother." Now we understand why Yaakov — having several wives — could not say "the sons of your mother"; but why could Yitzchak not say (as Yaakov did), "the sons of your father"? Thus, it appears that if one is not forced to use the father's name, it is better to use the mother's name.

6. See *Mikdash Melech* on *Zohar, Parshas Lech Lecha*, p. 84a, citing this Ashkenazic custom and supporting it. See also *Nishmas Avraham*, p. 212, note 13.
7. See *Darkei Chayim VeShalom* 1073.
8. See *Kisvei Eish*, op. cit. *Klalei Torah*, entry on *bakoshas rachamim*, note 4, who states that the custom of mentioning the mother's name when presenting a petition to *tzaddikim* derives from *Shabbos* 66b.
9. *Siddur Tehillat HaShem Nusach Ari — Chabad*.
10. Printed thus in various *siddurim*. See *Devar Yom BeYomo* — chart of *Halachah* and Custom, Customs of Belz (beginning of Cheshvan 5748).
11. See *Mekor Chesed*, note 1 on *Sefer Chassidim* 242:

Here, when mentioning the name of the deceased, our Rebbe specifies "the son of ..." in the feminine form. This is the custom when saying

6) In the *Yizkor* service, the name of the deceased is mentioned together with that of his mother.[13]

7) When engraving a tombstone, the name of the deceased is written, together with his father's name.[14]

8) When praying for a woman, if one does not know her mother's name, he should mention that she herself is "the mother of ...."[15]

---

    the memorial prayers and *E-l malei rachamim*. See *Berachos* 18b regarding Shmuel who went to Chatzar Maves and said, "I, son of Abba do pray..." He did not say "son of ..." in the feminine form. Thus, we see that he mentioned the name of his father's father, not his father's mother. Perhaps this is what *Ramban* refers to at the beginning of *Parshas Tazria*, where he says that the mother contributes the substance, and the father contributes the form. Thus, when praying for the health of the body, the mother is mentioned, but when praying for the soul of the deceased, the father's name is mentioned.

12. See *Mikdash Melech* on *Zohar, Parshas Lech Lecha*, p. 84, stating that this is the Ashkenazic custom. He justifies the custom on the basis that in this world we can only go by the majority. But in the World of Truth there are no doubts, and everything is revealed before Heaven. Thus, we can mention the father's name, for it is certain.

13. See *Kerem Chabad*, no. 1, p. 34, quoting the Rebbe's conversation on the second night of Shavuos 5730.

14. See *Darkei Chayim VeShalom* 977; *Beis Aharon*, Vol. 11, p. 536; *Responsa Melamed LeHo'il*, Vol. 1, ch. 53.

15. See *Midrash Tanchuma*, p. 201a: "But when he does not know the woman's mother's name, he should mention that she is the mother of ...; this will avail by mentioning the merits of her son's mother, in contrast to the verse, 'and do not erase the sin of his mother.'"

Chapter Thirty
Calling One's Father by His Name

1) It is forbidden to call one's father by his name.¹

2) If the father has the same name as other people, but it is an uncommon name that is not usually encountered; if the son wishes to address someone else with that name, he must change the name slightly.²

3) If the father's name is one that is commonly encountered, and the son wishes to address someone else with that name, it is permitted when not in the father's presence.³ Some say that it is permitted even when the father is present.⁴

4) If the son is asked, "Whose son are you?" he is permitted to answer, "I am the son of R. ...."⁵

---

1. See *Shulchan Aruch, Yoreh De'ah* 240:2, forbidding it both in his presence and not in his presence, even with a name that is not uncommon. See *Taz*, note 4.
2. *Shulchan Aruch*, loc. cit.
3. *Rama*, loc. cit.
4. *Drishah*, loc. cit.; *Bach*, loc. cit.; *Shach*, note 3.
5. See *Pischei Teshuvah*, loc. cit., note 2:
    In my opinion, if others ask him, "Whose son are you?" he is permitted to say, "I am the son of R. ...." A proof for this is found in *Yam Shel Shlomo, Kidushin*, no. 5, stating that *Rosh* mentioned his Rebbe *Maharam* by name, because there were other sages who were also his Rebbeim, and therefore he had to specify him by name. But regarding one's father, all agree that it is forbidden, for he has only one father. Indeed, *Tur* mentions his father by name, but he does so using the honorary title *Rosh*, meaning "the head of all of Israel."
    Thus, it appears that when it is necessary to specify by name, and otherwise people would not know whom he is referring to, it is permitted even in the case of his father. See also *Responsa Ohel Moshe*, Vol. 1, 25:3-4.

5) If the father is ill, and the son wishes to recite a *mi shabeirach* prayer in his behalf, some say that he should not state the father's name, but should say instead, "...my father *ben*...."[6]

---

6. See *Kal Bo HaChadash* on the laws of mourning.

CHAPTER THIRTY-ONE
CALLING ONE'S REBBE BY HIS NAME

1) It is forbidden for a disciple to call his Rebbe by his name, both while he is living, and after his death.[1]

2) If the Rebbe has the same name as other people, but it is an uncommon name that is not usually encountered; if the disciple wishes to address someone else with that name, it is forbidden unless he changes the name slightly.[2]

3) If the Rebbe's name is one that is commonly encountered, and the disciple wishes to address someone else with that name, it is permitted when not in the Rebbe's presence.[3]

4) All this is if he mentions his Rebbe's name alone. But, it is permitted to say "My Rebbe and master … ."[4] Some say that he may even say "My Rebbe …," without adding the title "master."[5]

5) Some say that what is permitted is specifically to say "My Rebbe …," but it is forbidden to say "…, my Rebbe."[6] Others disagree, and say that the order makes no difference; so long as an honorary title is included, it is permitted either way.[7]

---

1. *Shulchan Aruch, Yoreh De'ah* 242:15.
2. See *Kal Bo HaChadash* on the laws of mourning.
3. *Rama*, loc. cit.
4. Ibid.
5. Glosses of *Yad Avraham* loc. cit.
6. See *Parashas Derachim* quoted by *Birkei Yosef* loc. cit. However, consider the expression "Moshe *Rabbeinu*."
7. See *Or Yekaros* quoted by *Birkei Yosef* loc. cit.

6) Some maintain that the rule permitting one to refer to his Rebbe by name when including an honorary title, applies only when not in the Rebbe's presence. But in the Rebbe's presence, it is forbidden to call him by name even when adding an honorary title; in such case, he should simply say "My Rebbe."[8] Others disagree, saying that it makes no difference whether one is in his Rebbe's presence or not; if an honorary title is included, one may refer to his Rebbe by name.[9]

7) It is the common practice to say *Malbim, Mordechai, Alshich, Ya'avetz, Chida, Bachaye* etc., without adding an honorary title. Some maintain that this is not very respectful, even though these rabbis themselves referred to themselves by these names. However, if we add a definite article (*the Malbim*, etc.), this serves as a sort of honorary title.[10]

8) Some say that one may not call his Rebbe by his family surname, even when prefacing it with an honorary title, for it is like calling someone by a nickname.[11]

9) If the Rebbe is ill, and the disciple wishes to recite a *mi shabeirach* prayer in his behalf, including the patient's name in the *mi shebeirach* as is customary, some say that he should not pronounce his Rebbe's name vocally, but should instead think the name in his mind during the *mi shebeirach*.[12]

---

8. See *Shach*, loc. cit., note 24.
9. See *Birkei Yosef*, loc. cit.
10. See *Responsa Pe'as Sadecha*, Vol. 1, 34:4.
11. See *Pele Yoetz*; in his opinion, a family surname constitutes a nickname.
12. See *Kal Bo HaChadash* on the laws of mourning.

Chapter Thirty-Two
Whether a Husband and Wife Should Address Each Other by Name

1) Some have the custom that a couple do not address each other by name.[1]

2) Some say that the husband may address his wife by her name, but the wife should not address her husband by his name.[2]

3) Others say that there is no need to be particular about this, and they may address each other by name.[3]

---

1. See *Knesses HaGedolah, Even HaEzer* 1:1: "It is a common custom for married couples not to address each other by name." For a general overview of this subject, see *Ohel Rachel* (by R. Chayim Lieberman), Vol. 2, p. 346ff.; see also *Responsa HaMaor*, Vol. 1, p. 133; *Responsa Mevaser Tov* 79; addenda to *Zivchei Todah*, Vol. 1, on *Yoreh De'ah*. Note the Talmudic quote of R. Yosse (*Shabbos* 118b, *Gittin,* 52a): "Never in my life have I referred to my wife as 'my wife'; instead, I referred to my wife as 'my home.'" See *Responsa Minchas Elazar*, Vol. 3, ch. 13; *Darkei Chayim VeShalom* 1063; *Yad Shaul* on *Shulchan Aruch, Yoreh De'ah* 240:4.
2. See *Ohel Rachel*, loc. cit. See also *Radak's* commentary on *Bereishis* 17:15, "You shall not call her name Sarai":
    > It is the husband who calls his wife by her name, but the wife does not do so to her husband; she must address him with a lordly title of honor, and not by his name. Whenever someone is superior to another person, it is not fitting for the inferior one to address him by name, as is the case with one's father, Rebbe, or master.

    See also *HaYom Yom*, entry for 23 Shvat, "Mine says..."; *Sichah* of the Lubavitcher Rebbe of Shabbos *Parshas Shemos* 5713, paragraph 3.
3. This is the custom of the Ashkenazim; see *Sdei Chemed*, loc. cit. See also *Responsa Betzel HaChochmah*, Vol. 1, ch. 70.

Chapter Thirty-Three
If a Second Wife Has the Same Name As the First Wife

1) A man may not marry a second wife whose name is the same as his first wife.[1] Some, however, find a basis for leniency in this regard.[2]

2) Some say that this stringency applies only if the first wife died. But, if she was divorced, there is no objection.[3] Others say that even in the case of divorce, one should be strict about it.[4]

---

1. See *Chochmas HaNefesh* (by *Rokeach*), p. 24; *Shulchan HaEzer*, 1:12:6; addenda to the *Testament of R. Yehudah HaChassid*; *Bris Avos* 8:6; *Otzar HaPoskim*, end of ch. 2; *Testament of R. Yehudah HaChassid*, ch. 18; *Ta'amei HaMinhagim*, p. 423; *Otzar Kol Minhagei Yeshurun*, footnote on p. 280. The reason for this is that he will continue to think about the first wife, and there will thus never be any harmony between them. Or, one of them will die very soon because of it.
2. See *Az Nidberu*, Vol. 1, ch. 61.
3. See *Shulchan HaEzer*, 1:12:6; *Az Nidberu*, loc. cit.
4. Implied by *Shulchan HaEzer*, loc. cit.

CHAPTER THIRTY-FOUR
IF A SECOND HUSBAND HAS THE SAME NAME AS THE FIRST HUSBAND

1) A woman may not get married a second time to a husband with the same name as her first husband.[1]

2) Some say that this stringency applies only if the first husband died. But, if they were divorced, there is no objection.[2]

---

1. See *Chochmas HaNefesh* (by *Rokeach*), p. 24; *Shulchan HaEzer*, 1:12:6; addenda to the *Testament of R. Yehudah HaChassid*; *Bris Avos* 8:6; *Taamei HaMinhagim*, p. 423; *Otzar Kol Minhagei Yeshurun*, footnote on p. 280. The reason for this is that she will continue to think about the first husband, and there will thus never be any harmony between them. Or, one of them will die very soon because of it.
2. See *Shulchan HaEzer*, loc. cit.; *Az Nidberu*, Vol. 1, ch. 61.

CHAPTER THIRTY-FIVE
A DAUGHTER-IN-LAW AND MOTHER-IN-LAW WITH THE SAME NAME

1) It is written in the *Testament of R. Yehudah HaChassid*[1] that a man must not marry a woman whose name is the same as his mother's name.[2] And if he did marry such a woman, the name should be changed.[3]

---

1. *Testament of R. Yehudah HaChassid* 23; *Mishnas Chassidim* 5, quoting *AriZal*. See *Responsa Tzemach Tzedek, Even HaEzer* 143; *Piskei Dinim Tzemach Tzedek*, stating that his uncle R. Yehudah Leib said that the Alter Rebbe was more careful about identical names for a daughter-in-law and mother-in-law than about other precautions, because this one is also explained in *Mishnas Chassidim*, who cited only what was said by *AriZal*.

   See *Toras Chesed* 39; *Responsa Divrei Chayim, Even HaEzer* 8; *Mekor Chesed*, glosses on the *Testament of R. Yehudah HaChassid*, note 33; *Sdei Chemed*, entry on *Chasan VeKallah* 5, quoting *Mizmor LeDavid* 116, which lists things that *AriZal* cautioned about; among these, he writes that it is not good for a person to marry a woman with the same name as that of his mother; *Sdei Chemed* points out that though the *AriZal* says only that it is "not good," the possibility remains that there is also some sort of prohibition.

   See *Shulchan HaEzer*, 12:2 who writes that if one has a choice of two matches, both meeting with his approval; in one case, the woman and his mother have identical names, and in the second case, he and the woman's father have identical names; then, despite the fact that there are arguments for permitting even the former case, it appears preferable to permit the latter case, because some permit this outright, whereas identical names for the daughter-in-law and mother-in-law is treated more stringently by all authorities.
2. Several reasons have been offered for this prohibition, with numerous references for each reason: i) to avoid the evil eye; ii) because this would interfere with the honor due to one's mother; if the wife has the same name as his mother, and she gives birth to a daughter after his mother's death, he will be unable to honor his mother by naming the daughter after her; thus, if

2) Some say that there is no difference between the case of a first marriage and a second marriage — the same precaution applies to second marriages.⁴ Others disagree, saying that the precaution applies only to first marriages.⁵

3) Some say that the whole precaution applies only if the groom's mother is still living. But, if she has already died, none of this applies, and one may then marry a woman whose name is the same as his mother's name was.⁶

4) Some say that this precaution refers only to the case of three generations; i.e., there are three successive generations of marriages where the mothers-in-law and daughters-in-law all had the same name. But the first and second time, there is no objection.⁷

5) Some say that the *Testament* was intended exclusively for his own descendants, not for the general public.⁸

---

    the mother has two names, there is no objection, because he can honor her with the other name; iii) because it would cause him to call her by his mother's name, in his mother's presence, which is forbidden (see details above, ch. 30); iv) it is a decree designed to prevent a grave sin — it may happen that he will summon his wife (to have relations), and his mother will come instead.

3. A straightforward reading of the text of the *Testament* does not indicate who should change her name — the daughter-in-law, or the mother-in-law. *Sedei Chemed*, entry on *Chasan VeKallah* 7 writes that it makes no difference which one changes her name by adding a new name. Other sources state that the daughter-in-law is the one who should change her name by adding a name: *Responsa Tzemach Tzedek, Piskei Dinim* 116; *Pischei Teshuvah, Even HaEzer* 2:107; *Responsa Levush Mordechai, Even HaEzer* 44; *Mekor Chesed*, loc. cit., footnote 35; *Otzar HaPoskim*, loc. cit. 12.
4. *Shulchan HaEzer* 60:12:6; *Otzar HaPoskim*, loc. cit., 18.
5. *Responsa Pri HaSadeh*, Vol. 3, ch. 56, quoted in *Otzar HaPoskim*, loc. cit.
6. *Responsa Even HaRoshah* 31; *Yafeh LaLev*, Vol. 6, p. 6b; *Responsa Beis Shearim, Yoreh De'ah* 194.
7. *Chochmas Adam*, 123:13; see also *Sdei Chemed*, entry on *Chasan VeKallah* 5, and sources cited there.
8. *Responsa Noda BiYehudah* (2nd edition), ch. 79; see also *Responsa Chasam Sofer, Even HaEzer*, Vol. 1, ch. 116.

Chapter Thirty-Six
A Son-in-Law and Father-in-Law with the Same Name

1) It is written in the *Testament of R. Yehudah HaChassid* that a man must not marry a woman if the prospective father-in-law's name is the same as his own. And if he did marry such a woman, the name should be changed.[1]

2) Some do not pay attention to this precaution, because there are several passages in the Talmud that imply the opposite.[2]

3) Some say that the *Testament* was intended exclusively for his own descendants, not for the general public.[3]

---

1. *Testament of R. Yehudah HaChassid*, ch. 23, quoted in *Pischei Teshuvah, Even HaEzer* 2:107 and *Yoreh De'ah* 116:6. See *Sdei Chemed*, entry on *Chasan VeKallah* 5, citing *Sotah* 10b: Shmuel the Elder was the father-in-law of Shmuel bar Ami, indicating that in Talmudic times they were not careful to avoid a son-in-law and father-in-law having the same name; see ibid., quoting various texts that attempt to resolve this apparent contradiction. Additionally, *Yados Nedarim* cites *Menachos* 29b: Ramai bar Tari was the father-in-law of Rami bar Dikli, another case where the son-in-law and father-in-law had similar names.
2. See *Tzemach Tzedek, Piskei Dinim, Yoreh De'ah* 116, stating that since we find evidence to the contrary in the Talmud, we need not be scrupulous about it; see *Responsa Chasam Sofer, Even HaEzer*, Vol. 1, ch. 116, who states that if one has no personal objections to it, we have no objections about him.
3. *Responsa Noda BiYehudah* (2nd edition), ch. 79; see also *Responsa Chasam Sofer, Even HaEzer*, Vol. 1, ch. 116.

CHAPTER THIRTY-SEVEN
MECHUTANIM WITH THE SAME NAME

1) It is written in the *Testament of R. Yehudah HaChassid* that two men with the same names should not contract a marriage between their children.[1] Some say that if one of them has only one name, and the other has two names, we need not be careful about it;[2] also, if one is a *Kohen* and the other is a *Levi* or the like, we need not be careful about it.[3] Some say that the whole precaution applies only to an uncommon name, i.e., both of them have the same uncommon name. But with common names such as Avraham, Yitzchak, etc., we need not be careful about it.[4] Others are lenient about the entire matter, completely ignoring the fact that the two have the same name.[5]

---

1. *Testament of R. Yehudah HaChassid* 24: "Two men with the same names should not contract a marriage between their children"; (another version of the text: "...should not marry their two children to each other"); it is not clear whether he meant this only for his descendants, or for the public at large.
2. *Responsa Tzemach Tzedek, Even HaEzer* 143; *Sdei Chemed*, entry on *Chassan VeKallah* 7, quotes this, and states that although it deals with a case where the marriage has already taken place, the text implies that it may be done even in the first instance.
3. *Responsa Shem MiShimon, Even HaEzer* 6.
4. Ibid.
5. *Avnei Tzedek, Even HaEzer* 10 infers from the wording of the *Testament*, "Two men with the same names should not contract a marriage between their children," that it refers specifically to young children, where the fathers are the ones contracting the marriage. But in our countries the bride and groom are adults and capable of consent; therefore, they may marry each other, without regard to the fact that their fathers have identical names; moreover, the *Testament* itself is not clear whether it applies only to his descendants, or to everyone. In any such case of multiple doubt, we may be

lenient, by changing the name. When using this rationale, they must write in the engagement contract "the groom ... who is acting *on his own behalf* ... the bride ... who is acting *on her own behalf*," without mentioning the fathers.

See also *Heishiv Moshe* 69, who questions this article of the *Testament* from *Berachos* 42a: "Rav Yehudah was negotiating a match for his son with the family of Rav Yehudah *bar* Chavivi..."; thus we find two *mechutanim* with the same name. He speculates that perhaps one of them was usually called by some nickname, but the Talmud mentioned only the sacred name. *Mekor Chesed* on the *Testament* 36 speculates that *"bar* Chavivi" was part of his own name; thus, he had an additional name, and in such case we may be lenient.

CHAPTER THIRTY-EIGHT
MECHUTANOS WITH THE SAME NAME

1) It is written in the *Testament of R. Yehudah HaChassid* that two men with the same names should not contract a marriage between their children.¹ Some interpret this precaution as applying only to male *mechutanim*, but there is no objection to female *mechutanos* with identical names.² Many great authorities ruled as a matter of law that it is permitted.³

---

1. *Testament of R. Yehudah HaChassid* 24.
2. See *Responsa Even Yekarah* (1st edition), *Even HaEzer* 15, who permits it because there is a double doubt: whether the *Testament* applies only to his descendants, or to everyone; and whether this precaution also applies to the mothers. *Responsa Beis Naftali* 12 and *Avnei Tzedek, Even HaEzer* 6 similarly permit it.
   Cf. *Avnei Tzedek*, loc. cit., who writes that even according to our text of the *Testament*, "two men with the same names should not contract a marriage between their children," it does not admonish us that a person should not marry a wife if the *mechutanim* or *mechutanos* would have identical names; the admonition is specifically that people with identical names should not contract a marriage between their children. Thus, only the *mechutanim* are forbidden, for they are the ones contracting the marriage. But regarding the *mechutanos*, the matter does not depend upon them, and their names do not appear in the engagement contract as undertaking the obligations; nor are the names of the *mechutanos* written in the *kesubah*. Thus, there is no reason to object.
   Sdei Chemed, entry on *Chasan VeKallah* 10 quotes *Ruach Chayim* saying that there is no objection to the women having the same name; *Sdei Chemed* questions this conclusion — if the reason is because of the evil eye, then woman also need to protect their life, and why would women ignore the evil eye? Also, op. cit. 17, where he writes that we need worry about the evil eye only in the case of *mechutanim*, whose names are mentioned in the *kesubah* and in the *shul* during the *mi shebeirach*, but this does not apply to *mechutanos*. He objects to this reasoning, because the text of the *Testament* does not

explicitly exclude *mechutanos*; thus, we have no right to guess at the reason and to draw conclusions based on this.
3. See *Shulchan HaEzer* 2, who states that inasmuch as many great authorities have ruled that it is permitted, we may be lenient, especially if there is some additional mitigating factor. See the sources cited in the previous footnote, and *Responsa Teshuvos VeHanhagos* 731.

CHAPTER THIRTY-NINE
SYMBOLIC REFERENCE TO THE AUTHOR'S NAME IN THE TITLE OF HIS *SEFER*

1) Some have the custom when writing a *sefer* to include a symbolic reference to the author's name in the title.[1]

---

1. See the Introduction to *Rokeiach* (by R. Elazar of Garmise):
    Every person should record his name in his *sefer*; for example, *Tanna deVei Eliyahu*, which begins with the word *Vayegaresh*, being the numeric equivalent of *Tanna deVei Eliyahu*. *Midrash Tadshei* begins with the word *Tadshei*, being the numeric equivalent of *zeh R. Pinchas ben Yair*. *Midrash Bereishis Rabbah* begins with *VeEhyeh Sha'ashuim*, the equivalent of *zeh R. Hosheia Rabbah*. *Pirkei deRabbi Eliezer* begins with *Mi yemalel gevuros HaShem*, the equivalent of *Eliezer ben Horkenus*. *Seder Olam* begins with *MeAdam*, the equivalent of *Yosse*.
    Therefore, he named his own *sefer Rokeiach*, the numeric equivalent of his name. It remains unclear why he writes that *Tanna deVei Eliyahu* and *Pirkei deRabbi Eliezer* begin with the numeric equivalent of the authors' names, when in fact the names themselves appear in the titles of their works (unlike *Midrash Rabbah* and *Midrash Tadshei*). Similarly, *Tzemach Tzedek* is the numeric equivalent of the author's name.
    Some give the reason for this custom as following the rule of quoting things in the name of the one who said them, as the Sages rule in *Avos* 6:6, "Whoever says a thing in the name of its author brings redemption to the world, as it is stated, 'And Esther told the king in the name of Mordechai.'"
    Others write that the reason is in keeping with the adage, "his lips vibrate along in the grave," as the Sages said (*Yerushalmi Shekalim* 7:2), "Shimon ben Nezira said in the name of R. Yitzchak: whenever a Torah passage by any Torah scholar is quoted in this world, his lips vibrate along in the grave, as it is said (*Shir HaShirim* 7:10) 'the lips of those who sleep move.'"
    See also *Yevamos* 96b: "Is it possible for someone to dwell in both worlds [at once]? this means that David said to the Holy One: 'Master of the world: may it be Your will that people quote something they heard from my mouth in this world...'" *Tosafos* comments: "When his soul is on High, his lips move in the grave as if he is speaking, and thus the person exists in both worlds at once."

2) Some have the custom to include a symbolic reference to the author's name specifically in the first word of the title.[2]

Others say that the reason is to ensure that his memory will last through future generations, as the Sages said in *Sanhedrin* 93b: What is the meaning of "I will give him an everlasting name that shall never be cut off"? (*Yeshayahu* 56:2); R. Tanchum quoted what Bar Kapara expounded in Tzipori: "this refers to the book of *Daniel*, that was called by his own name." See also *Zohar, Parshas Vayechi* 217b: "I have come before you to make three requests; one of them is that when you speak words of Torah, let the words that I said be mentioned, and say them in my name, so that my name will be remembered."

2. See *Rokeiach*, op. cit., discussing *Midrash Tadshei*.

CHAPTER FORTY
USING TITLES

1) It is best to refrain from using too many honorary titles when writing to an individual person; this practice borders on sycophancy by the one who writes such titles, and it borders on conceit by the one to whom they are written.[1]

2) Some authorities take exception to the practice of certain rabbis who append החופק״ק ["who dwells here, in the holy community of ..."] and the like to their signatures, for this borders on conceit. Others find excuse for this practice, based on the verse in *Parshas Yisro*, "...that [Moshe] was dwelling there, at the mountain of G-d."[2]

3) If one's father bears the title *Rabbeinu*, he should not sign his name "I, ... ben *Rabbeinu HaKadosh* (or *HaChassid*)," for it is written, "Let others praise you, not your own mouth."[3] Some say that this applies only if he signs his name thus for his own glory. But if he signs thus for his father's honor, there is no objection.[4]

---

1. See the Introduction to *Responsa R. Akiva Eiger*; *Responsa Salmas Chayim* (by R. Chayim Sonenfeld), Vol. 2, ch. 1: "Do not write any titles, even those that you are accustomed to; if you do write titles, I will not reply."

    See also *Likkutei Sichos*, Vol. 1, p. 138; Vol. 2, p. 504: "I received a letter from a certain Jew, in which he relates that my father-in-law the Rebbe once wrote to him, 'I don't use titles lightly; if I address someone in writing as "my intimate comrade," or "my staunch comrade," that is how things truly are.' Even if the recipient of the letter is at present not up to that standard, he eventually will be."
2. See *Responsa Chasam Sofer*, Vol. 6, ch. 59.
3. See *Sefer Chassidim* 522.
4. See *Responsa Pe'as Sadecha*, Vol. 1, ch. 115: "This is to discourage the authors who mention the great authorities of previous generations, and, if they are their descendants, they mention this fact. [This is wrong,] unless their intent

4) Some say that the entire practice of calling oneself by the title *HaRav* would be improper, were it not for the fact that refraining from using the title might denigrate the honor of the rabbinate in general.⁵

6) Some are careful to add the title *HaKadosh* ["the holy"] when mentioning the name of certain great Jewish figures; others are not particular about it.⁶

5) Some do not add the words נשמתו עדן ["his soul is in *Gan Eden*"] or זכר צדיק לברכה ["may the *tzaddik's* memory be a blessing"] when mentioning the name of a departed *tzaddik*. The reason is that a memorial can apply only to something that is liable to be forgotten. But if one feels that the *tzaddik* remains continuously with him, then there is no possibility of forgetting.⁷

---

    is for the sake of Heaven; i.e., if the grandson is a prominent person, then 'the crown of the elders is their grandchildren.'"

5.   See *Responsa Pe'as Sadecha*, loc. cit. See *Pesachim* 86b:
    R. Huna son of R. Nasan arrived at the home of R. Nachman *bar* Yitzchak. They said to him, "What is your name?" He replied, "Rav Huna." They than said to him, "Master, please sit on the couch.." He sat; they gave him a cup [of wine]. He took it all at once, drank it in two gulps, and did not turn his face aside. They said to him, "For what reason do you call yourself 'Rav' Huna?" He replied to them, "That is my name" (*Rashi explains:* "I have been called Rav Huna since my early youth").

6.   See *Likkutei Sichos*, Vol. 2, p. 508.

7.   See *Likkutei Sichos*, Vol. 18, p. 462:
    On Simchas Torah 5691 my father-in-law the Rebbe said that whenever he speaks of his father, the Rebbe Rashab, he does not use the title נשמתו עדן; the reason he gave was, "I am not an address writer." For the same reason,, when I speak of my father-in-law the Rebbe, I do not add the title נשמתו עדן, or even זכר צדיק לברכה.

    The Rebbe mentioned additional reasons to refrain from using these titles:

    i. Regarding the tittle נשמתו עדן: (a) who among us knows how to specify whether the title נשמתו עדן refers to the Lower *Gan Eden*, the Upper *Gan Eden*, or even higher levels (to which there is no end)? (b) for what purpose should we distance him from ourselves? He certainly does not wish to be separated from us, and indeed he is here with us. This is mentioned in *Yevamos* 96b [see previous chapter, note 1], "his lips vibrate along in the grave," meaning that he is here also in this world. *Tosafos*, loc. cit. writes that it refers to the *yeshivah* on High. This means that there are two kinds of *yeshivah*; in the *yeshivah* of the lower worlds, matters pertaining to the lower worlds are studied; in the *yeshivah* of the Upper World, matters pertaining to the Upper Worlds are studied. Now even before his *histalkus*, he was in the *yeshivah* of the Upper Worlds, but this fact was concealed; only his presence in the *yeshivah* of the lower worlds was visible. But after the *histalkus*, the opposite is true. What is visible is that he is in the *yeshivah* of the Upper Worlds, and what is concealed is his presence in the *yeshivah* of the lower worlds. Thus, the fact of the matter is that there has been essentially no change at all; the only difference is in what is concealed, and what is visible.

    ii. Regarding the title זכר צדיק לברכה: the term "memory" is applicable only to something far away, which is liable to be forgotten. But in our case, where forgetting (G-d forbid) is not possible, there is no need for any "memorial," the same way that there is no need to memorialize a living person.

CHAPTER FORTY-ONE
CALLING UP A PERSON TO THE TORAH BY HIS NAME

1) It is necessary to call a person to go up to the Torah reading.[1] Some, however, say that it is sufficient to indicate by some sign that the person is to go up, and it is not necessary to call him by name.[2]

2) It is a long-standing custom to call him by his own name and that of his father. A reference to this is the verse, "Behold, I have called by name Betzalel *ben* Uri...."[3] He should not be called by the general address, "Arise, *Kohen*," or the like.[4]

3) When calling a *Kohen* or a *Levi* to go up to the Torah, he is called by his own name and that of his father, and the word *Kohen* or *Levi* is added.[5]

---

1. See *Rosh* on *Megillah*, ch. 3; *Beis Yosef, Orach Chayim* 139:3, "the head of the congregation or the *chazan* of the congregation may not begin reading until they instruct him, saying, 'Read!'" Similarly, "Whoever reads [publicly] from the Torah without having been instructed to do so is likened to someone who has an adolescent daughter who is taken by anyone who desires to take her." Even the President of the congregation must not read on his own initiative.
2. *Darkei Moshe, Orach Chayim* 135:68, quoting *Mordechai*.
3. *Sefer Matamim* (revised edition), entry on *keriah*, note 12.
4. *Rosh* on *Gittin*, ch. *HaSholeiach*, note 7: "The Jews of Germany are accustomed to the gentiles addressing them by non-Jewish names, so that they were compelled to change their names. But a distinction should be made for the sake of the Torah; when the people gather in *shul*, they should be called by names given by their parents."

    See *Siddur Rav Amram Gaon*, p. 139: "When the *chazan* begins, he calls the *Kohen*, addressing him as follows: 'Arise, R ... ben ...,' and so on, for the other people called up."
5. *Darkei Chayim VeShalom*, loc. cit.

4) In some Sephardic communities the custom is to refrain from calling him by name. They merely call "Arise *Kohen*" etc. The *shamash* approaches the one who is being called up, and informs him that it is he to whom they refer.[6] This is also the custom of several congregations in Yerushalayim.[7]

5) In some congregations the custom is that on Shabbos and festival days, people are called up by name, but on weekdays they are called up by the generic phrase, "Arise *Kohen*" etc.[8]

6) In some communities the custom is that all are called up by name except the seventh person; he is called up in generic terms, without mentioning his name.[9]

7) When calling up a Jew whose mother is Jewish but whose father is a gentile, he should be called up by his maternal grandfather's name;[10] they should not use a substitute name for his father's name.[11]

8) Someone whose father has deserted the Jewish religion, is called up to the Torah by his own name and the name of his paternal grandfather.[12]

---

6. *Kaf HaChayim* 139:9; *Responsa Chayim Sho'al*, Vol. 1, ch. 13, et. al. The reason given is that in case he has some reason for not wishing to go up to the Torah, the *shamash* can call someone else, without his being included in the category of "he who is called and does not go up."
7. *Responsa Chayim Sho'al*, op. cit.
8. See *Zeh HaShulchan*, p. 233; at the *Minchah* Service on Shabbos, there is no fixed custom. This custom is observed in all cities of Algeria.
9. See *Eliyahu Rabbah* 141:6.
10. *Rama, Orach Chayim* 139:3; see also *Nachalas Tzvi*, 122.
11. See *Teshuvas HaRosh*, end of ch. 17; *Mevaser Tov, Even HaEzer* 74; *Chasam Sofer, Even HaEzer*, Vol. 2, ch. 41.
12. *Rama, Orach Chayim* 139:3; *Pri Megadim* questions what should be done in case the paternal grandfather is also an apostate; should he be called by the name of his paternal grandfather's father? He rules that this should not be done, for such a name would invalidate a *get*; the adage that "grandchildren are considered as children" does not extend beyond these generations.

CHAPTER FORTY-TWO
ADDRESSING PEOPLE NAMED SHALOM AND THE LIKE, IN THE BATHHOUSE

1) Some have the custom to refrain from addressing by name in the bathhouse a person named Shalom, for Shalom is one of G-d's Names.[1]

2) Some say that in addition, he should not even be addressed in the vernacular language; for Shalom is G-d's Name, and holy things may not be said [in the bathhouse] even in the vernacular language.[2]

3) Some are also careful to avoid addressing someone with the name Yehudah by name in the bathhouse; instead, they address him in the vernacular, "Lion."[3]

---

1. See *Magen Avraham* 84:2; *Machtzis HaShekel*, loc. cit. See *Taamei HaMinhagim*, p. 504, stating that the *Gaon* R.Z. refused to employ a bathhouse attendant named Shalom.
2. See *Pri Chadash* 84, who quotes *Bach's* ruling that a person named Shalom may be addressed in the vernacular; he disagrees, concluding that it is obviously forbidden.
    See *Kesef Mishneh* on *Hilchos Kerias Shema* 3:5 "I am greatly puzzled by the text of *Rambam*, for he failed to mention that it is forbidden to say 'Shalom' in the bathhouse; that law is stated explicitly by R. Hamnuna in *Shabbos* 10b ... and we find no authority who disagrees."
3. See *Orchos Chayim* 84, quoting *Yafeh LaLev*.

CHAPTER FORTY-THREE
MISCELLANEOUS

1) Some say that several people who have the same name should not live in the same house.[1]

2) Two people who have the same name, or names of the same numeric value, should treat each other with love.[2]

3) A charm recommended for one who has no children, is to utter a vow that he will name his first son Shimon, after Rabbi Shimon bar Yochai.[3]

4) The name of one's Rebbe can help him as much as any of the Holy Names.[4]

5) Each person should find for himself a number corresponding to [his name and] one of the unifying Names of G-d, [to have in mind] when signing his name.[5]

---

1. *Sefer Chassidim* 477; *Testament of R. Yehudah HaChassid* 34; *Knesses HaGedolah, Yoreh De'ah* 116; *Otzer HaPoskim, Even HaEzer* end of ch. 2.
2. *Devash LeFi* (by *Chida*), letter *kuf*.
3. See *Taamei HaMinhagim*, p. 263.
4. *Taamei HaMinhagim*, footnote on p. 303.
5. *Divrei Torah* (Munkatch), Vol. 2, ch. 87; *Darkei Chayim VeShalom* 1066, citing the source as *Yerushalmi, Chagigah* 3:5.

CHAPTER FORTY-FOUR
RECITING A VERSE BEGINNING AND ENDING WITH THE SAME LETTERS AS ONE'S NAME

1) It is proper to recite each day a verse beginning and ending with the same letters as one's name, or else a verse in which the name is mentioned.[1]

2) If one has several names, he should recite a verse for each name.[2]

3) Our custom is to recite this verse several times a day, at the conclusion of the *Shemoneh Esreh* prayer.[3]

---

1. See the parenthetical statement in *Rashi* on *Michah* 6:9, "This teaches us that whoever recites each day a verse beginning and ending with the same letters that his name begins and ends with, will be saved from *Gehinnom* by the Torah." But, *Likkutei Sichos*, Vol. 14, p. 227 cites those who question whether the parenthetical statement was written by *Rashi* himself, or by someone else.

    Mishpat Tzedek (quoted in addenda to *Taamei HaMinhagim*, section on Prayer, note 90) quotes a *Kabbalistic Siddur* that it is advisable to recite the verse corresponding to one's name before departing on a journey, or engaging in commercial affairs, studying Torah, or any other undertaking.
2. See *Segulas Yisrael*, letter *shin*, note 91.
3. In many *siddurim*, after *Shemoneh Esreh*, is printed (citing *Shaloh*) that a charm to prevent forgetting one's name on the Day of Judgement is to recite before *yihiyu leratzon* a verse from the Torah, the Prophets, or the Holy Scriptures, beginning and ending with the same letters as one's name. *Likkutei Sichos*, Vol. 14, p. 227 cites *Rashi* on *Michah* 6:9 [see above, footnote 1]. He says that this *Rashi* refers to the custom cited in many *siddurim* (and this is also the custom of *Chabad*) to recite verses ...; "several times a day" means that the verse is recited at the end of *E-lohai Netzor*:

    > Regarding what is to be done in actual practice, I asked my father-in-law the Rebbe; he replied that when he began studying Torah and saying the prayers, his father (the Rebbe Rashab) instructed him to

4) A woman should also recite such verses beginning and ending with the same letters as her name.[4]

5) The verse that one recites can even be taken from those chapters of *Tehillim* that are not recited on festive days.[5]

6) Some are accustomed also to recite verses beginning and ending with the same letters as their Rebbe's name.[6]

7) When praying for a sick person, one recites verses of *Tehillim* that begin with the same letter as his name.[7]

---

    recite at the end of the prayer the verses ... [*Tehillim* 138:8 and 107:14, corresponding to the names Yosef Yitzchak] ... this was to be said at each prayer, every day.

    See *Kitzur Shaloh*, essay on "Reward and Punishment," mentioning that a person may forget his name at the Time of Judgement, but he mentions not a word about reciting verses corresponding to his name to prevent his forgetting. In op. cit., "Procedure for Changing a Name," this is mentioned explicitly: "The wicked do not know their name in the grave, and so they are beaten brutally. But whoever recites every day of his life a verse beginning with the same letter as his name ... it serves as a charm not to forget his name." However, this passage is not copied from *Shaloh* himself, but is an insertion by the compiler. After this, he inserts a list of the verses, and he himself writes that it was taken from the *sefer Ben Tzion*, not from *Shaloh*.

    Kerem Shlomo quotes *Beis Yosef* that it is advisable to recite a verse from ... before saying *yihiyu leratzon*. I searched extensively, and was unable to find any hint of such a thing in *Beis Yosef*; perhaps he refers to some other *sefer*.

    Az Nidberu, Vol. 4, ch. 45 discusses whether these verses constitute an unlawful interruption in the prayer, since many of the verses contain praises and not prayers. He concludes that if this were recited only as a charm, that might be true. But since they are recited as a form of prayer, verses of praise are also considered prayer.

4. See *Likkutei Sichos*, op. cit.
5. See *Responsa Divrei Ephraim Eliezer* (Yolles), ch. 37.
6. See letter of the Lubavitcher Rebbe, printed in *Teshuvos U'Biurim Yagdil Torah* (1:10): "several of the chassidim had the custom to recite — before *yihiyu leratzon* — the verse corresponding to their name, and also the verse corresponding to the name of my father-in-law the Rebbe."
7. See end of *Kitzur Shaloh*, in the procedure for changing a name, "I heard from a Polish Rabbi that he once knew of a case of a great misfortune that befell a certain city (may we be spared); their rabbi instructed them that each person should recite verses of *Tehillim* corresponding to the letters of the city's name; e.g., if the city's name is Rothenburg, they should recite the verses beginning with the letter *reish*, then all the verses beginning with the letter *vav*, then all the verses beginning with the letter *tes*, and so on."

Chapter Forty-Five
List of Verses Corresponding to Names of Men and Women

א

א-א : אָנָּא יְהוָה הוֹשִׁיעָה נָּא אָנָּא יְהוָה הַצְלִיחָה נָּא (תהלים קיח, כה)

א-ב : אַשְׁרֵי הָאִישׁ אֲשֶׁר לֹא הָלַךְ בַּעֲצַת רְשָׁעִים וּבְדֶרֶךְ חַטָּאִים לֹא עָמָד וּבְמוֹשַׁב לֵצִים לֹא יָשָׁב (תהלים א, א)

א-ג : אֵלֶּה אֶזְכְּרָה וְאֶשְׁפְּכָה עָלַי נַפְשִׁי כִּי אֶעֱבֹר בַּסָּךְ אֶדַּדֵּם עַד בֵּית אֱלֹהִים בְּקוֹל רִנָּה וְתוֹדָה הָמוֹן חוֹגֵג (תהלים מב, ה)

א-ד : אַזְכִּירָה שִׁמְךָ בְּכָל דֹּר וָדֹר עַל כֵּן עַמִּים יְהוֹדוּךָ לְעוֹלָם וָעֶד (תהלים מה, יח)

א-ה : אַשְׁרֵי מַשְׂכִּיל אֶל דָּל בְּיוֹם רָעָה יְמַלְּטֵהוּ יְהוָה (תהלים מא, ב)

א-ו : אַשְׁרֵי שֶׁאֵל יַעֲקֹב בְּעֶזְרוֹ שִׂבְרוֹ עַל יְהוָה אֱלֹהָיו (תהלים קמו, ה)

א-ז : אֵלֶּה בְּנֵי אֲבִיחַיִל בֶּן חוּרִי בֶּן יָרוֹחַ בֶּן גִּלְעָד בֶּן מִיכָאֵל בֶּן יְשִׁישַׁי בֶּן יַחְדּוֹ בֶּן בּוּז (דברי הימים-א ה, יד)

א-ח : אִם תַּחֲנֶה עָלַי מַחֲנֶה לֹא יִירָא לִבִּי אִם תָּקוּם עָלַי מִלְחָמָה בְּזֹאת אֲנִי בוֹטֵחַ (תהלים כז, ג)

א-ט : אַךְ הוּא צוּרִי וִישׁוּעָתִי מִשְׂגַּבִּי לֹא אֶמּוֹט (תהלים סב, ז)

א-י : אֲמָרַי הַאֲזִינָה יְהוָה בִּינָה הֲגִיגִי (תהלים ה, ב)

א-כ : אָמַרְתְּ לַיהוָה אֲדֹנָי אָתָּה טוֹבָתִי בַּל עָלֶיךָ (תהלים טז, ב)

א-ל : אֶרֶץ רָעָשָׁה אַף שָׁמַיִם נָטְפוּ מִפְּנֵי אֱלֹהִים זֶה סִינַי מִפְּנֵי אֱלֹהִים אֱלֹהֵי יִשְׂרָאֵל (תהלים סח, ט)

א-מ : אַתָּה הוּא יְהוָה הָאֱלֹהִים אֲשֶׁר בָּחַרְתָּ בְּאַבְרָם וְהוֹצֵאתוֹ מֵאוּר כַּשְׂדִּים וְשַׂמְתָּ שְּׁמוֹ אַבְרָהָם (נחמיה ט, ז)

א-נ : אֵלֶיךָ יְהוָה אֶקְרָא וְאֶל אֲדֹנָי אֶתְחַנָּן (תהלים ל, ט)

א-ס : אֹרַח לַצַּדִּיק מֵישָׁרִים יָשָׁר מַעְגַּל צַדִּיק תְּפַלֵּס (ישעיה כו, ז)

א-ע : אָמַר בְּלִבּוֹ בַּל אֶמּוֹט לְדֹר וָדֹר אֲשֶׁר לֹא בְרָע (תהלים י, ו)

א-פ : אֱמֶת מֵאֶרֶץ תִּצְמָח וְצֶדֶק מִשָּׁמַיִם נִשְׁקָף (תהלים פה, יב)

א-צ : אֹהֵב צְדָקָה וּמִשְׁפָּט חֶסֶד יְהוָה מָלְאָה הָאָרֶץ (תהלים לג, ה)

א-ק : אֲשֶׁר כָּרַת אֶת אַבְרָהָם וּשְׁבוּעָתוֹ לְיִשְׂחָק (תהלים קה, ט)

א-ר : אֵלֶּה בָרֶכֶב וְאֵלֶּה בַסּוּסִים וַאֲנַחְנוּ בְּשֵׁם יְהוָה אֱלֹהֵינוּ נַזְכִּיר (תהלים כ, ח)

א-ש : אֲשֶׁר יַחְדָּו נַמְתִּיק סוֹד בְּבֵית אֱלֹהִים נְהַלֵּךְ בְּרָגֶשׁ (תהלים נה, טו)
א-ת : אַשְׁרֵי שֹׁמְרֵי מִשְׁפָּט עֹשֵׂה צְדָקָה בְכָל עֵת (תהלים קו, ג)

ב

ב-א : בֵּית אַהֲרֹן בִּטְחוּ בַיהֹוָה עֶזְרָם וּמָגִנָּם הוּא (תהלים קטו, י)
ב-ב : בְּנִדָבָה אֶזְבְּחָה לָּךְ אוֹדֶה שִּׁמְךָ יְהֹוָה כִּי טוֹב (תהלים נד, ח)
ב-ג : בְּנָיָהוּ בֶן יְהוֹיָדָע בֶּן אִישׁ חַיִל רַב פְּעָלִים מִן קַבְצְאֵל הוּא הִכָּה אֵת שְׁנֵי אֲרִיאֵל מוֹאָב וְהוּא יָרַד וְהִכָּה אֶת הָאֲרִי בְּתוֹךְ הַבּוֹר בְּיוֹם הַשָּׁלֶג (דברי הימים-א יא, כב)
ב-ד : בְּכָל יוֹם אֲבָרְכֶךָּ וַאֲהַלְלָה שִׁמְךָ לְעוֹלָם וָעֶד (תהלים קמה, ב)
ב-ה : בַּעֲבוּר יִשְׁמְרוּ חֻקָּיו וְתוֹרֹתָיו יִנְצֹרוּ הַלְלוּיָהּ (תהלים קה, מה)
ב-ו : בְּךָ בָּטְחוּ אֲבֹתֵינוּ בָּטְחוּ וַתְּפַלְּטֵמוֹ (תהלים כב, ה)
ב-ז : בְּיוֹם קָרָאתִי וַתַּעֲנֵנִי תַּרְהִבֵנִי בְנַפְשִׁי עֹז (תהלים קלח, ג)
ב-ח : בֵּית רְשָׁעִים יִשָּׁמֵד וְאֹהֶל יְשָׁרִים יַפְרִיחַ (משלי יד, יא)
ב-ט : בְּאֹרַח צְדָקָה אֲהַלֵּךְ בְּתוֹךְ נְתִיבוֹת מִשְׁפָּט (משלי ח, כ)
ב-י : בִּנְאוֹת דֶּשֶׁא יַרְבִּיצֵנִי עַל מֵי מְנֻחוֹת יְנַהֲלֵנִי (תהלים כג, ב)
ב-כ : בָּרוּךְ אַתָּה יְהֹוָה לַמְּדֵנִי חֻקֶּיךָ (תהלים קיט, יב)
ב-ל : בְּמַקְהֵלוֹת בָּרְכוּ אֱלֹהִים אֲדֹנָי מִמְּקוֹר יִשְׂרָאֵל (תהלים סח, כז)
ב-מ : בְּכָל הָאָרֶץ יָצָא קַוָּם וּבִקְצֵה תֵבֵל מִלֵּיהֶם לַשֶּׁמֶשׁ שָׂם אֹהֶל בָּהֶם (תהלים יט, ה)
ב-נ : בָּרוּךְ יְהֹוָה אֱלֹהֵי יִשְׂרָאֵל מֵהָעוֹלָם וְעַד הָעוֹלָם אָמֵן וְאָמֵן (תהלים מא, יד)
ב-ס : בּוֹנֵה יְרוּשָׁלִַם יְהֹוָה נִדְחֵי יִשְׂרָאֵל יְכַנֵּס (תהלים קמז, ב)
ב-ע : בְּחֶסֶד וֶאֱמֶת יְכֻפַּר עָוֹן וּבְיִרְאַת יְהֹוָה סוּר מֵרָע (משלי טז, ו)
ב-פ : בַּיּוֹם הַשְּׁלִישִׁי יֵאָכֵל וּמִמָּחֳרָת וְהַנּוֹתָר עַד יוֹם הַשְּׁלִישִׁי בָּאֵשׁ יִשָּׂרֵף (ויקרא יט, ו)
ב-צ : בְּרוּכִים אַתֶּם לַיהֹוָה עֹשֵׂה שָׁמַיִם וָאָרֶץ (תהלים קטו, טו)
ב-ק : בַּיּוֹם הַשְּׁלִישִׁי וַיִּשָּׂא אַבְרָהָם אֶת עֵינָיו וַיַּרְא אֶת הַמָּקוֹם מֵרָחֹק (בראשית כב, ד)
ב-ר : בְּנוֹת מְלָכִים בְּיִקְּרוֹתֶיךָ נִצְּבָה שֵׁגַל לִימִינְךָ בְּכֶתֶם אוֹפִיר (תהלים מה, י)
ב-ש : בְּרוּחַ קָדִים תְּשַׁבֵּר אֳנִיּוֹת תַּרְשִׁישׁ (תהלים מח, ח)
ב-ת : בְּיָדְךָ אַפְקִיד רוּחִי פָּדִיתָה אוֹתִי יְהֹוָה אֵל אֱמֶת (תהלים לא, ו)

ג

ג-א : גַּם הוּא לִי לִישׁוּעָה כִּי לֹא לְפָנָיו חָנֵף יָבוֹא (איוב יג, טז)
ג-ב : גַּם עַבְדְּךָ נִזְהָר בָּהֶם בְּשָׁמְרָם עֵקֶב רָב (תהלים יט, יב)
ג-ד : גַּאֲוַת אָדָם תַּשְׁפִּילֶנּוּ וּשְׁפַל רוּחַ יִתְמֹךְ כָּבוֹד (משלי כט, כג)
ג-ה : גּוֹל עַל יְהֹוָה דַּרְכֶּךָ וּבְטַח עָלָיו וְהוּא יַעֲשֶׂה (תהלים לז, ה)
ג-ו : גָּדוֹל כְּבוֹדוֹ בִּישׁוּעָתֶךָ הוֹד וְהָדָר תְּשַׁוֶּה עָלָיו (תהלים כא, ו)
ג-ח : גֶּבֶר חָכָם בַּעוֹז וְאִישׁ דַּעַת מְאַמֶּץ כֹּחַ (משלי כד, ה)
ג-י : גַּם עֵדֹתֶיךָ שַׁעֲשֻׁעָי אַנְשֵׁי עֲצָתִי (תהלים קיט, כד)
ג-כ : גִּבּוֹר בָּאָרֶץ יִהְיֶה זַרְעוֹ דּוֹר יְשָׁרִים יְבֹרָךְ (תהלים קיב, ב)
ג-ל : גַּם אֲנִי אוֹדְךָ בִכְלִי נֶבֶל אֲמִתְּךָ אֱלֹהָי אֲזַמְּרָה לְךָ בְכִנּוֹר קְדוֹשׁ יִשְׂרָאֵל (תהלים עא, כב)

ג-מ: גְּדֹלִים מַעֲשֵׂי יְהֹוָה דְּרוּשִׁים לְכָל חֶפְצֵיהֶם (תהלים קיא, ב)
ג-נ: גַּם בְּנֵי אָדָם גַּם בְּנֵי אִישׁ יַחַד עָשִׁיר וְאֶבְיוֹן (תהלים מט, ג)
ג-ע: גָּבְהֵי שָׁמַיִם מַה תִּפְעָל עֲמֻקָּה מִשְּׁאוֹל מַה תֵּדָע (איוב יא, ח)
ג-פ: גְּדָל חֵמָה נֹשֵׂא עֹנֶשׁ כִּי אִם תַּצִּיל וְעוֹד תּוֹסִף (משלי יט, יט)
ג-צ: גְּבוּל שַׂמְתָּ בַּל יַעֲבֹרוּן בַּל יְשׁוּבוּן לְכַסּוֹת הָאָרֶץ (תהלים קד, ט)
ג-ק: גַּם אֹתָם הִקְדִּישׁ הַמֶּלֶךְ דָּוִיד לַיהֹוָה עִם הַכֶּסֶף וְהַזָּהָב אֲשֶׁר נָשָׂא מִכָּל הַגּוֹיִם מֵאֱדוֹם וּמִמּוֹאָב וּמִבְּנֵי עַמּוֹן וּמִפְּלִשְׁתִּים וּמֵעֲמָלֵק (דברי הימים-א יח, יא)
ג-ר: גָּדוֹל יְהֹוָה וּמְהֻלָּל מְאֹד וְלִגְדֻלָּתוֹ אֵין חֵקֶר (תהלים קמה, ג)
ג-ש: גַּם אֹתָם הִקְדִּישׁ הַמֶּלֶךְ דָּוִד לַיהֹוָה עִם הַכֶּסֶף וְהַזָּהָב אֲשֶׁר הִקְדִּישׁ מִכָּל הַגּוֹיִם אֲשֶׁר כִּבֵּשׁ (שמואל-ב ח, יא)
ג-ת: גָּרְסָה נַפְשִׁי לְתַאֲבָה אֶל מִשְׁפָּטֶיךָ בְכָל עֵת (תהלים קיט, כ)

ד

ד-א: דַּבֵּר אֶל אַהֲרֹן וְאֶל בָּנָיו לֵאמֹר זֹאת תּוֹרַת הַחַטָּאת בִּמְקוֹם אֲשֶׁר תִּשָּׁחֵט הָעֹלָה תִּשָּׁחֵט הַחַטָּאת לִפְנֵי יְהֹוָה קֹדֶשׁ קָדָשִׁים הִוא (ויקרא ו, יח)
ד-ב: דִּרְשׁוּ יְהֹוָה בְּהִמָּצְאוֹ קְרָאֻהוּ בִּהְיוֹתוֹ קָרוֹב (ישעיה נה, ו)
ד-ד: דִּרְשׁוּ יְהֹוָה וְעֻזּוֹ בַּקְּשׁוּ פָנָיו תָּמִיד (תהלים קה, ד)
ד-ה: דְּאָגָה בְלֶב אִישׁ יַשְׁחֶנָּה וְדָבָר טוֹב יְשַׂמְּחֶנָּה (משלי יב, כה)
ד-י: דְּרָכֶיךָ יְהֹוָה הוֹדִיעֵנִי אֹרְחוֹתֶיךָ לַמְּדֵנִי (תהלים כה, ד)
ד-כ: דָּמִינוּ אֱלֹהִים חַסְדֶּךָ בְּקֶרֶב הֵיכָלֶךָ (תהלים מח, י)
ד-ל: דָּן יָדִין עַמּוֹ כְּאַחַד שִׁבְטֵי יִשְׂרָאֵל (בראשית מט, טז)
ד-מ: דְּרָכֶיהָ דַרְכֵי נֹעַם וְכָל נְתִיבוֹתֶיהָ שָׁלוֹם (משלי ג, יז)
ד-נ: דַּבֵּר אֶל בְּנֵי יִשְׂרָאֵל וְאָמַרְתָּ אֲלֵהֶם כִּי אַתֶּם עֹבְרִים אֶת הַיַּרְדֵּן אֶל אֶרֶץ כְּנָעַן (במדבר לג, נא)
ד-פ: דְּעוּ אֵפוֹ כִּי אֱלוֹהַּ עִוְּתָנִי וּמְצוּדוֹ עָלַי הִקִּיף (איוב יט, ו)
ד-צ: דַּבְּרוּ אֶל בְּנֵי יִשְׂרָאֵל לֵאמֹר זֹאת הַחַיָּה אֲשֶׁר תֹּאכְלוּ מִכָּל הַבְּהֵמָה אֲשֶׁר עַל הָאָרֶץ (ויקרא יא, ב)
ד-ר: דָּן וְנַפְתָּלִי גָּד וְאָשֵׁר (שמות א, ד)
ד-ש: דַּבֵּר אֶל בְּנֵי יִשְׂרָאֵל לֵאמֹר בַּחֹדֶשׁ הַשְּׁבִיעִי בְּאֶחָד לַחֹדֶשׁ יִהְיֶה לָכֶם שַׁבָּתוֹן זִכְרוֹן תְּרוּעָה מִקְרָא קֹדֶשׁ (ויקרא כג, כד)
ד-ת: דַּבְּרוּ אֶל כָּל עֲדַת יִשְׂרָאֵל לֵאמֹר בֶּעָשֹׂר לַחֹדֶשׁ הַזֶּה וְיִקְחוּ לָהֶם אִישׁ שֶׂה לְבֵית אָבֹת שֶׂה לַבָּיִת (שמות יב, ג)

ה

ה-א: הַצּוּר תָּמִים פָּעֳלוֹ כִּי כָל דְּרָכָיו מִשְׁפָּט אֵל אֱמוּנָה וְאֵין עָוֶל צַדִּיק וְיָשָׁר הוּא (דברים לב, ד)
ה-ב: הֲלֹא אֱלֹהִים יַחֲקָר זֹאת כִּי הוּא יֹדֵעַ תַּעֲלֻמוֹת לֵב (תהלים מד, כב)
ה-ג: הַקְּדִרִים מִנִּי קָרַח עָלֵימוֹ יִתְעַלֶּם שָׁלֶג (איוב ו, טז)
ה-ד: הֵמָּה כָּרְעוּ וְנָפָלוּ וַאֲנַחְנוּ קַּמְנוּ וַנִּתְעוֹדָד (תהלים כ, ט)

WHAT'S IN A NAME

ה-ה: הָפַכְתָּ מִסְפְּדִי לְמָחוֹל לִי פִּתַּחְתָּ שַׂקִּי וַתְּאַזְּרֵנִי שִׂמְחָה (תהלים ל, יב)
ה-ו: הוֹלֵךְ תָּמִים וּפֹעֵל צֶדֶק וְדֹבֵר אֱמֶת בִּלְבָבוֹ (תהלים טו, ב)
ה-ז: הָבוּ לַיהוָה מִשְׁפְּחוֹת עַמִּים הָבוּ לַיהוָה כָּבוֹד וָעֹז (תהלים צו, ז)
ה-ח: הַמְקָרֶה בַמַּיִם עֲלִיּוֹתָיו הַשָּׂם עָבִים רְכוּבוֹ הַמְהַלֵּךְ עַל כַּנְפֵי רוּחַ (תהלים קד, ג)
ה-ט: הֲנֹטַע אֹזֶן הֲלֹא יִשְׁמָע אִם יֹצֵר עַיִן הֲלֹא יַבִּיט (תהלים צד, ט)
ה-י: הָאֵל הַמְאַזְּרֵנִי חָיִל וַיִּתֵּן תָּמִים דַּרְכִּי (תהלים יח, לג)
ה-כ: הָאִירָה פָנֶיךָ עַל-עַבְדֶּךָ הוֹשִׁיעֵנִי בְחַסְדֶּךָ (תהלים לא, יז)
ה-ל: הַקְשִׁיבָה לְקוֹל שַׁוְעִי מַלְכִּי וֵאלֹהָי כִּי אֵלֶיךָ אֶתְפַּלָּל (תהלים ה, ג)
ה-מ: הַנֶּחֱמָדִים מִזָּהָב וּמִפַּז רָב וּמְתוּקִים מִדְּבַשׁ וְנֹפֶת צוּפִים (תהלים יט, יא)
ה-נ: הַר אֱלֹהִים הַר בָּשָׁן הַר גַּבְנֻנִּים הַר בָּשָׁן (תהלים סח, טז)
ה-ס: הִנֵּה אַשְׁרֵי אֱנוֹשׁ יוֹכִחֶנּוּ אֱלוֹהַּ וּמוּסַר שַׁדַּי אַל-תִּמְאָס (איוב ה, יז)
ה-ע: הַשָּׁמַיִם מְסַפְּרִים כְּבוֹד אֵל וּמַעֲשֵׂה יָדָיו מַגִּיד הָרָקִיעַ (תהלים יט, ב)
ה-פ: הַחַיָּה וְכָל בְּהֵמָה רֶמֶשׂ וְצִפּוֹר כָּנָף (תהלים קמח, י)
ה-צ: הִשְׁתַּחֲווּ לַיהוָה בְּהַדְרַת קֹדֶשׁ חִילוּ מִפָּנָיו כָּל הָאָרֶץ (תהלים צו, ט)
ה-ק: הַשְׁלֵךְ עַל יְהוָה יְהָבְךָ וְהוּא יְכַלְכְּלֶךָ לֹא יִתֵּן לְעוֹלָם מוֹט לַצַּדִּיק (תהלים נה, כג)
ה-ר: הַיָּם רָאָה וַיָּנֹס הַיַּרְדֵּן יִסֹּב לְאָחוֹר (תהלים קיד, ג)
ה-ש: הָבוּ לַיהוָה כְּבוֹד שְׁמוֹ הִשְׁתַּחֲווּ לַיהוָה בְּהַדְרַת קֹדֶשׁ (תהלים כט, ב)
ה-ת: הַלְלוּ אֶת יְהוָה מִן הָאָרֶץ תַּנִּינִים וְכָל תְּהֹמוֹת (תהלים קמח, ז)

ו

ו-א: וְלֹא נָסוֹג מִמֶּךָּ תְּחַיֵּנוּ וּבְשִׁמְךָ נִקְרָא (תהלים פ, יט)
ו-ב: וַאֲנִי אַגִּיד לְעֹלָם אֲזַמְּרָה לֵאלֹהֵי יַעֲקֹב (תהלים עה, י)
ו-ג: וַיְחִי רְעוּ שְׁתַּיִם וּשְׁלֹשִׁים שָׁנָה וַיּוֹלֶד אֶת שְׂרוּג (בראשית יא, כ)
ו-ד: וַאֲנִי כְּזַיִת רַעֲנָן בְּבֵית אֱלֹהִים בָּטַחְתִּי בְחֶסֶד אֱלֹהִים עוֹלָם וָעֶד (תהלים נב, י)
ו-ה: וְלֹא אָמְרוּ הָעֹבְרִים בִּרְכַּת יְהוָה אֲלֵיכֶם בֵּרַכְנוּ אֶתְכֶם בְּשֵׁם יְהוָה (תהלים קכט, ח)
ו-ו: וַיהוָה לְעוֹלָם יֵשֵׁב כּוֹנֵן לַמִּשְׁפָּט כִּסְאוֹ (תהלים ט, ח)
ו-ז: וַיַּעַשׂ הַמֶּלֶךְ כִּסֵּא שֵׁן גָּדוֹל וַיְצַפֵּהוּ זָהָב מוּפָז (מלכים-א י, יח)
ו-ח: וְהָיָה כְּעֵץ שָׁתוּל עַל פַּלְגֵי מָיִם אֲשֶׁר פִּרְיוֹ יִתֵּן בְּעִתּוֹ וְעָלֵהוּ לֹא יִבּוֹל וְכֹל אֲשֶׁר יַעֲשֶׂה יַצְלִיחַ (תהלים א, ג)
ו-ט: וַיְבָרֲכֵם וַיִּרְבּוּ מְאֹד וּבְהֶמְתָּם לֹא יַמְעִיט (תהלים קז, לח)
ו-י: וְאַתָּה יְהוָה מָגֵן בַּעֲדִי כְּבוֹדִי וּמֵרִים רֹאשִׁי (תהלים ג, ד)
ו-כ: וַאֲנִי בְּרֹב חַסְדְּךָ אָבוֹא בֵיתֶךָ אֶשְׁתַּחֲוֶה אֶל הֵיכַל קָדְשְׁךָ בְּיִרְאָתֶךָ (תהלים ה, ח)
ו-ל: וְאַתָּה קָדוֹשׁ יוֹשֵׁב תְּהִלּוֹת יִשְׂרָאֵל (תהלים כב, ד)
ו-מ: וְהוּא יִשְׁפֹּט תֵּבֵל בְּצֶדֶק יָדִין לְאֻמִּים בְּמֵישָׁרִים (תהלים ט, ט)
ו-נ: וּבָרוּךְ שֵׁם כְּבוֹדוֹ לְעוֹלָם וְיִמָּלֵא כְבוֹדוֹ אֶת כָּל הָאָרֶץ אָמֵן וְאָמֵן (תהלים עב, יט)
ו-ס: וַיִּלְקְטוּ אֹתוֹ בַּבֹּקֶר בַּבֹּקֶר אִישׁ כְּפִי אָכְלוֹ וְחַם הַשֶּׁמֶשׁ וְנָמָס (שמות טז, כא)

ו-ע: וְאַף אֱלֹהִים עָלָה בָּהֶם וַיַּהֲרֹג בְּמִשְׁמַנֵּיהֶם וּבַחוּרֵי יִשְׂרָאֵל הִכְרִיעַ (תהלים עח, לא)

ו-פ: וְכַתּוֹתִי מִפָּנָיו צָרָיו וּמְשַׂנְאָיו אֶגּוֹף (תהלים פט, כג)

ו-צ: וְעַתָּה מְלָכִים הַשְׂכִּילוּ הִוָּסְרוּ שֹׁפְטֵי אָרֶץ (תהלים ב, י)

ו-ק: וְכָל קַרְנֵי רְשָׁעִים אֲגַדֵּעַ תְּרוֹמַמְנָה קַרְנוֹת צַדִּיק (תהלים עה, יא)

ו-ר: וַיַּסַּע כַּצֹּאן עַמּוֹ וַיְנַהֲגֵם כַּעֵדֶר בַּמִּדְבָּר (תהלים עח, נ)

ו-ש: וַיַּנְחֵם בֶּעָנָן יוֹמָם וְכָל הַלַּיְלָה בְּאוֹר אֵשׁ (תהלים עח, יד)

ו-ת: וִיחִי עוֹד לָנֶצַח לֹא יִרְאֶה הַשָּׁחַת (תהלים מט, י)

ז

ז-א: זֹאת עֲבֹדַת מִשְׁפְּחֹת הַגֵּרְשֻׁנִּי לַעֲבֹד וּלְמַשָּׂא (במדבר ד, כד)

ז-ב: זֵכֶר צַדִּיק לִבְרָכָה וְשֵׁם רְשָׁעִים יִרְקָב (משלי י, ז)

ז-ד: זֹאת אֲשֶׁר לַלְוִיִּם מִבֶּן חָמֵשׁ וְעֶשְׂרִים שָׁנָה וָמַעְלָה יָבוֹא לִצְבֹא צָבָא בַּעֲבֹדַת אֹהֶל מוֹעֵד (במדבר ח, כד)

ז-ה: זֹאת מְנוּחָתִי עֲדֵי עַד פֹּה אֵשֵׁב כִּי אִוִּתִיהָ (תהלים קלב, יד)

ז-ו: זִכְרוּ נִפְלְאֹתָיו אֲשֶׁר עָשָׂה מֹפְתָיו וּמִשְׁפְּטֵי פִיהוּ (דברי הימים-א טז, יב)

ז-ז: זֶה הַדָּבָר אֲשֶׁר דִּבֶּר יְהוָה אֶל מוֹאָב מֵאָז (ישעיה טז, יג)

ז-ח: זָכַרְתִּי יָמִים מִקֶּדֶם הָגִיתִי בְכָל פָּעֳלֶךָ בְּמַעֲשֵׂה יָדֶיךָ אֲשׂוֹחֵחַ (תהלים קמג, ה)

ז-ט: זְבוּבֵי מָוֶת יַבְאִישׁ יַבִּיעַ שֶׁמֶן רוֹקֵחַ יָקָר מֵחָכְמָה מִכָּבוֹד סִכְלוּת מְעָט (קהלת י, א)

ז-י: זַרְעוֹ לְעוֹלָם יִהְיֶה וְכִסְאוֹ כַשֶּׁמֶשׁ נֶגְדִּי (תהלים פט, לז)

ז-כ: זָכַרְתִּי בַלַּיְלָה שִׁמְךָ יְהוָה וָאֶשְׁמְרָה תּוֹרָתֶךָ (תהלים קיט, נה)

ז-ל: זֹאת חֻקַּת הַתּוֹרָה אֲשֶׁר צִוָּה יְהוָה לֵאמֹר דַּבֵּר אֶל בְּנֵי יִשְׂרָאֵל וְיִקְחוּ אֵלֶיךָ פָרָה אֲדֻמָּה תְּמִימָה אֲשֶׁר אֵין בָּהּ מוּם אֲשֶׁר לֹא עָלָה עָלֶיהָ עֹל (במדבר יט, ב)

ז-מ: זֹבֵחַ תּוֹדָה יְכַבְּדָנְנִי וְשָׂם דֶּרֶךְ אַרְאֶנּוּ בְּיֵשַׁע אֱלֹהִים (תהלים נ, כג)

ז-נ: זְבוּלֻן לְחוֹף יַמִּים יִשְׁכֹּן וְהוּא לְחוֹף אֳנִיּוֹת וְיַרְכָתוֹ עַל צִידֹן (בראשית מט, יג)

ז-ס: זְבוּלֻן לֹא הוֹרִישׁ אֶת יוֹשְׁבֵי קִטְרוֹן וְאֶת יוֹשְׁבֵי נַהֲלֹל וַיֵּשֶׁב הַכְּנַעֲנִי בְּקִרְבּוֹ וַיִּהְיוּ לָמַס (שופטים א, ל)

ז-פ: זְרַמְתָּם שֵׁנָה יִהְיוּ בַּבֹּקֶר כֶּחָצִיר יַחֲלֹף (תהלים צ, ה)

ז-צ: זַמְּרוּ יְהוָה כִּי גֵאוּת עָשָׂה מוּדַעַת זֹאת בְּכָל הָאָרֶץ (ישעיה יב, ה)

ז-ק: זָרַח בַּחֹשֶׁךְ אוֹר לַיְשָׁרִים חַנּוּן וְרַחוּם וְצַדִּיק (תהלים קיב, ד)

ז-ר: זָכַר לְעוֹלָם בְּרִיתוֹ דָּבָר צִוָּה לְאֶלֶף דּוֹר (תהלים קה, ח)

ז-ש: זְכָר עָנְיִי וּמְרוּדִי לַעֲנָה וָרֹאשׁ (איכה ג, יט)

ז-ת: זֶה הַיָּם גָּדוֹל וּרְחַב יָדָיִם שָׁם רֶמֶשׂ וְאֵין מִסְפָּר חַיּוֹת קְטַנּוֹת עִם גְּדֹלוֹת (תהלים קד, כה)

ח

ח-א: חִדְלוּ לָכֶם מִן הָאָדָם אֲשֶׁר נְשָׁמָה בְּאַפּוֹ כִּי בַמֶּה נֶחְשָׁב הוּא (ישעיה ב, כב)

ח-ב: חַכְלִילִי עֵינַיִם מִיָּיִן וּלְבֶן שִׁנַּיִם מֵחָלָב (בראשית מט, יב)

ח-ד: חַנּוּן וְרַחוּם יְהוָה אֶרֶךְ אַפַּיִם וּגְדָל חָסֶד (תהלים קמה, ח)
ח-ה: חַרְבָּם תָּבוֹא בְלִבָּם וְקַשְּׁתוֹתָם תִּשָּׁבַרְנָה (תהלים לז, טו)
ח-ו: חֶסֶד וֶאֱמֶת נִפְגָּשׁוּ צֶדֶק וְשָׁלוֹם נָשָׁקוּ (תהלים פה, יא)
ח-ז: חָנֵּנוּ יְהוָה חָנֵּנוּ כִּי רַב שָׂבַעְנוּ בוּז (תהלים קכג, ג)
ח-ח: חָכָם יָרֵא וְסָר מֵרָע וּכְסִיל מִתְעַבֵּר וּבוֹטֵחַ (משלי יד, טז)
ח-ט: חִילוּ מִלְּפָנָיו כָּל-הָאָרֶץ אַף תִּכּוֹן תֵּבֵל בַּל תִּמּוֹט (דברי הימים-א טז, ל)
ח-י: חֲבָלִים נָפְלוּ לִי בַּנְּעִמִים אַף נַחֲלָת שָׁפְרָה עָלָי (תהלים טז, ו)
ח-כ: חֲצוֹת לַיְלָה אָקוּם לְהוֹדוֹת לָךְ עַל מִשְׁפְּטֵי צִדְקֶךָ (תהלים קיט, סב)
ח-ל: חָדְלוּ פְרָזוֹן בְּיִשְׂרָאֵל חָדֵלּוּ עַד שַׁקַּמְתִּי דְּבוֹרָה שַׁקַּמְתִּי אֵם בְּיִשְׂרָאֵל (שופטים ה, ז)
ח-מ: חֹנֶה מַלְאַךְ יְהוָה סָבִיב לִירֵאָיו וַיְחַלְּצֵם (תהלים לד, ח)
ח-נ: חֶשְׁבּוֹן וְכָל עָרֶיהָ אֲשֶׁר בַּמִּישֹׁר דִּיבֹן וּבָמוֹת בַּעַל וּבֵית בַּעַל מְעוֹן (יהושע יג, יז)
ח-ס: חֹרֶיהָ וְאֵין שָׁם מְלוּכָה יִקְרָאוּ וְכָל שָׂרֶיהָ יִהְיוּ אָפֶס (ישעיה לד, יב)
ח-פ: חָרַשׁ בַּרְזֶל מַעֲצָד וּפָעַל בַּפֶּחָם וּבַמַּקָּבוֹת יִצְּרֵהוּ וַיִּפְעָלֵהוּ בִּזְרוֹעַ כֹּחוֹ גַּם רָעֵב וְאֵין כֹּחַ לֹא שָׁתָה מַיִם וַיִּיעָף (ישעיה מד, יב)
ח-צ: חָשַׁךְ מִשְּׁחוֹר תָּאֳרָם לֹא נִכְּרוּ בַּחוּצוֹת צָפַד עוֹרָם עַל-עַצְמָם יָבֵשׁ הָיָה כָעֵץ (איכה ד, ח)
ח-ק: חָזֵה הֲוֵית עַד דִּי כָרְסָוָן רְמִיו וְעַתִּיק יוֹמִין יְתִב לְבוּשֵׁהּ כִּתְלַג חִוָּר וּשְׂעַר רֵאשֵׁהּ כַּעֲמַר נְקֵא כָּרְסְיֵהּ שְׁבִיבִין דִּי נוּר גַּלְגִּלּוֹהִי נוּר דָּלִק (דניאל ז, ט)
ח-ר: חֶמְאַת בָּקָר וַחֲלֵב צֹאן עִם חֵלֶב כָּרִים וְאֵילִים בְּנֵי-בָשָׁן וְעַתּוּדִים עִם חֵלֶב כִּלְיוֹת חִטָּה וְדַם עֵנָב תִּשְׁתֶּה חָמֶר (דברים לב, יד)
ח-ש: חֹפֵר גּוּמָּץ בּוֹ יִפּוֹל וּפֹרֵץ גָּדֵר יִשְּׁכֶנּוּ נָחָשׁ (קהלת י, ח)
ח-ת: חֲמִשִּׁים לֻלָאֹת עָשָׂה בַּיְרִיעָה הָאֶחָת וַחֲמִשִּׁים לֻלָאֹת עָשָׂה בִּקְצֵה הַיְרִיעָה אֲשֶׁר בַּמַּחְבֶּרֶת הַשֵּׁנִית מַקְבִּילֹת הַלֻּלָאֹת אַחַת אֶל אֶחָת (שמות לו, יב)

ט

ט-א: טוֹב יַנְחִיל בְּנֵי בָנִים וְצָפוּן לַצַּדִּיק חֵיל חוֹטֵא (משלי יג, כב)
ט-ב: טָמוּן בָּאָרֶץ חַבְלוֹ וּמַלְכֻּדְתּוֹ עֲלֵי נָתִיב (איוב יח, י)
ט-ד: טַפֵּנוּ נָשֵׁינוּ מִקְנֵנוּ וְכָל בְּהֶמְתֵּנוּ יִהְיוּ שָׁם בְּעָרֵי הַגִּלְעָד (במדבר לב, כו)
ט-ה: טָמְנוּ-גֵאִים פַּח לִי וַחֲבָלִים פָּרְשׂוּ רֶשֶׁת לְיַד-מַעְגָּל מֹקְשִׁים שָׁתוּ לִי סֶלָה (תהלים קמ, ו)
ט-ו: טַעֲמוּ וּרְאוּ כִּי-טוֹב יְהוָה אַשְׁרֵי הַגֶּבֶר יֶחֱסֶה בּוֹ (תהלים לד, ט)
ט-ח: טוֹב מְלֹא כַף נָחַת מִמְּלֹא חָפְנַיִם עָמָל וּרְעוּת רוּחַ (קהלת ד, ו)
ט-ט: טוֹב אִישׁ חוֹנֵן וּמַלְוֶה יְכַלְכֵּל דְּבָרָיו בְּמִשְׁפָּט (תהלים קיב, ה)
ט-י: טוּב טַעַם וָדַעַת לַמְּדֵנִי כִּי בְמִצְוֹתֶיךָ הֶאֱמָנְתִּי (תהלים קיט, סו)
ט-כ: טוֹב וְיָשָׁר יְהוָה עַל כֵּן יוֹרֶה חַטָּאִים בַּדָּרֶךְ (תהלים כה, ח)
ט-ל: טוֹב רָשׁ הוֹלֵךְ בְּתֻמּוֹ מֵעִקֵּשׁ שְׂפָתָיו וְהוּא כְסִיל (משלי יט, א)
ט-מ: טוֹב לַחֲסוֹת בַּיהוָה מִבְּטֹחַ בָּאָדָם (תהלים קיח, ח)

ט-נ: טוֹב לְהֹדוֹת לַיהוָה וּלְזַמֵּר לְשִׁמְךָ עֶלְיוֹן (תהלים צב, ב)
ט-ס: טוֹב שֶׁבֶת בְּאֶרֶץ מִדְבָּר מֵאֵשֶׁת מִדְיָנִים וָכָעַס (משלי כא, יט)
ט-ע: טוֹב יָפִיק רָצוֹן מֵיהוָה וְאִישׁ מְזִמּוֹת יַרְשִׁיעַ (משלי יב, ב)
ט-פ: טוֹב לִי תוֹרַת-פִּיךָ מֵאַלְפֵי זָהָב וָכָסֶף (תהלים קיט, עב)
ט-ר: טוֹב אֶרֶךְ אַפַּיִם מִגִּבּוֹר וּמֹשֵׁל בְּרוּחוֹ מִלֹּכֵד עִיר (משלי טז, לב)
ט-ש: טוֹבָה חָכְמָה עִם נַחֲלָה וְיֹתֵר לְרֹאֵי הַשָּׁמֶשׁ (קהלת ז, יא)
ט-ת: טוֹבָה תּוֹכַחַת מְגֻלָּה מֵאַהֲבָה מְסֻתָּרֶת (משלי כז, ה)

י

י-א: יִתֶּן-לְךָ כִלְבָבֶךָ וְכָל עֲצָתְךָ יְמַלֵּא (תהלים כ, ה)
י-ב: יַעַנְךָ יְהוָה בְּיוֹם צָרָה יְשַׂגֶּבְךָ שֵׁם אֱלֹהֵי יַעֲקֹב (תהלים כ, ב)
י-ג: יַעֲלוּ שָׁמַיִם יֵרְדוּ תְהוֹמוֹת נַפְשָׁם בְּרָעָה תִתְמוֹגָג (תהלים קז, כו)
י-ד: יֹאכְלוּ עֲנָוִים וְיִשְׂבָּעוּ יְהַלְלוּ יְהוָה דֹּרְשָׁיו יְחִי לְבַבְכֶם לָעַד (תהלים כב, כז)
י-ה: יְהוָה הַצִּילָה נַפְשִׁי מִשְּׂפַת שֶׁקֶר מִלָּשׁוֹן רְמִיָּה (תהלים קכ, ב)
י-ו: יִרְאַת יְהוָה טְהוֹרָה עוֹמֶדֶת לָעַד מִשְׁפְּטֵי יְהוָה אֱמֶת צָדְקוּ יַחְדָּו (תהלים יט, י)
י-ז: יְהוָה קָנָנִי רֵאשִׁית דַּרְכּוֹ קֶדֶם מִפְעָלָיו מֵאָז (משלי ח, כב)
י-ח: יִפְרַח בְּיָמָיו צַדִּיק וְרֹב שָׁלוֹם עַד בְּלִי יָרֵחַ (תהלים עב, ז)
י-ט: יָדִין עַמְּךָ בְצֶדֶק וַעֲנִיֶּיךָ בְמִשְׁפָּט (תהלים עב, ב)
י-י: יְהוָה לִי בְּעֹזְרָי וַאֲנִי אֶרְאֶה בְשֹׂנְאָי (תהלים קיח, ז)
י-כ: יִשְׁלַח עֶזְרְךָ מִקֹּדֶשׁ וּמִצִּיּוֹן יִסְעָדֶךָּ (תהלים כ, ג)
י-ל: יְמִין יְהוָה רוֹמֵמָה יְמִין יְהוָה עֹשָׂה חָיִל (תהלים קיח, טז)
י-מ: יַעְלְזוּ חֲסִידִים בְּכָבוֹד יְרַנְּנוּ עַל מִשְׁכְּבוֹתָם (תהלים קמט, ה)
י-נ: יָשֵׂם נְהָרוֹת לְמִדְבָּר וּמֹצָאֵי מַיִם לְצִמָּאוֹן (תהלים קז, לג)
י-ס: יַד חָרוּצִים תִּמְשׁוֹל וּרְמִיָּה תִּהְיֶה לָמַס (משלי יב, כד)
י-ע: יָחֹס עַל דַּל וְאֶבְיוֹן וְנַפְשׁוֹת אֶבְיוֹנִים יוֹשִׁיעַ (תהלים עב, יג)
י-פ: יְהוָה יִגְמֹר בַּעֲדִי יְהוָה חַסְדְּךָ לְעוֹלָם מַעֲשֵׂי יָדֶיךָ אַל תֶּרֶף (תהלים קלח, ח)
י-צ: יְבָרְכֵנוּ אֱלֹהִים וְיִירְאוּ אוֹתוֹ כָּל אַפְסֵי אָרֶץ (תהלים סז, ח)
י-ק: יוֹצִיאֵם מֵחֹשֶׁךְ וְצַלְמָוֶת וּמוֹסְרוֹתֵיהֶם יְנַתֵּק (תהלים קז, יד)
י-ר: יֹאמְרוּ גְּאוּלֵי יְהוָה אֲשֶׁר גְּאָלָם מִיַּד צָר (תהלים קז, ב)
י-ש: יִפֹּל מִצִּדְּךָ אֶלֶף וּרְבָבָה מִימִינֶךָ אֵלֶיךָ לֹא יִגָּשׁ (תהלים צא, ז)
י-ת: יוֹם לְיוֹם יַבִּיעַ אֹמֶר וְלַיְלָה לְלַיְלָה יְחַוֶּה דָּעַת (תהלים יט, ג)

כ

כ-א: כִּי הִטָּה אָזְנוֹ לִי וּבְיָמַי אֶקְרָא (תהלים קטז, ב)
כ-ב: כִּי לֹא יִטֹּשׁ יְהוָה עַמּוֹ וְנַחֲלָתוֹ לֹא יַעֲזֹב (תהלים צד, יד)
כ-ד: כָּל אֵלֶּה אַנְשֵׁי מִלְחָמָה עֹדְרֵי מַעֲרָכָה בְּלֵבָב שָׁלֵם בָּאוּ חֶבְרוֹנָה לְהַמְלִיךְ אֶת דָּוִיד עַל כָּל יִשְׂרָאֵל וְגַם כָּל שֵׁרִית יִשְׂרָאֵל לֵב אֶחָד לְהַמְלִיךְ אֶת דָּוִיד (דברי הימים-א יב, לט)
כ-ה: כִּי אִם בְּתוֹרַת יְהוָה חֶפְצוֹ וּבְתוֹרָתוֹ יֶהְגֶּה יוֹמָם וָלָיְלָה (תהלים א, ב)

כ־ו: כִּי־אַתָּה תְּבָרֵךְ צַדִּיק יְהוָה כַּצִּנָּה רָצוֹן תַּעְטְרֶנּוּ (תהלים ה, יג)
כ־ז: כִּי־תְקַדְּמֶנּוּ בִּרְכוֹת טוֹב תָּשִׁית לְרֹאשׁוֹ עֲטֶרֶת פָּז (תהלים כא, ד)
כ־ח: כִּי־יִקַּח אִישׁ אִשָּׁה חֲדָשָׁה לֹא יֵצֵא בַּצָּבָא וְלֹא־יַעֲבֹר עָלָיו לְכָל־דָּבָר נָקִי יִהְיֶה לְבֵיתוֹ שָׁנָה אֶחָת וְשִׂמַּח אֶת־אִשְׁתּוֹ אֲשֶׁר־לָקָח (דברים כד, ה)
כ־ט: כִּי־הַמֶּלֶךְ בֹּטֵחַ בַּיהוָה וּבְחֶסֶד עֶלְיוֹן בַּל־יִמּוֹט (תהלים כא, ח)
כ־י: כִּי כָל־מִשְׁפָּטָיו לְנֶגְדִּי וְחֻקֹּתָיו לֹא־אָסִיר מֶנִּי (תהלים יח, כג)
כ־כ: כִּי־חַסְדְּךָ לְנֶגֶד עֵינָי וְהִתְהַלַּכְתִּי בַּאֲמִתֶּךָ (תהלים כו, ג)
כ־ל: כִּי מֶלֶךְ כָּל־הָאָרֶץ אֱלֹהִים זַמְּרוּ מַשְׂכִּיל (תהלים מז, ח)
כ־מ: כְּאַיָּל תַּעֲרֹג עַל־אֲפִיקֵי־מָיִם כֵּן נַפְשִׁי תַעֲרֹג אֵלֶיךָ אֱלֹהִים (תהלים מב, ב)
כ־נ: כִּי־הָיִיתָ עֶזְרָתָה לִּי וּבְצֵל כְּנָפֶיךָ אֲרַנֵּן (תהלים סג, ח)
כ־ס: כִּי נֹכַח יְהוָה דַּרְכֵי־אִישׁ וְכָל־מַעְגְּלֹתָיו מְפַלֵּס (משלי ה, כא)
כ־ע: כִּי טוֹב יוֹם בַּחֲצֵרֶיךָ מֵאָלֶף בָּחַרְתִּי הִסְתּוֹפֵף בְּבֵית אֱלֹהַי מִדּוּר בְּאָהֳלֵי־רֶשַׁע (תהלים פד, יא)
כ־פ: כִּי־בְחַנְתָּנוּ אֱלֹהִים צְרַפְתָּנוּ כִּצְרָף־כָּסֶף (תהלים סו, י)
כ־צ: כִּי־יְהוָה עֶלְיוֹן נוֹרָא מֶלֶךְ גָּדוֹל עַל־כָּל־הָאָרֶץ (תהלים מז, ג)
כ־ק: כִּי־לְעוֹלָם לֹא־יִמּוֹט לְזֵכֶר עוֹלָם יִהְיֶה צַדִּיק (תהלים קיב, ו)
כ־ר: כִּי־עִמְּךָ מְקוֹר חַיִּים בְּאוֹרְךָ נִרְאֶה־אוֹר (תהלים לו, י)
כ־ש: כָּל־הַנֶּפֶשׁ הַבָּאָה לְיַעֲקֹב מִצְרַיְמָה יֹצְאֵי יְרֵכוֹ מִלְּבַד נְשֵׁי בְנֵי־יַעֲקֹב כָּל־נֶפֶשׁ שִׁשִּׁים וָשֵׁשׁ (בראשית מו, כו)
כ־ת: כֹּל אֲשֶׁר־חָפֵץ יְהוָה עָשָׂה בַּשָּׁמַיִם וּבָאָרֶץ בַּיַּמִּים וְכָל־תְּהוֹמוֹת (תהלים קלה, ו)

ל

ל־א: לְדָוִד אֵלֶיךָ יְהוָה נַפְשִׁי אֶשָּׂא (תהלים כה, א)
ל־ב: לֶךְ־נָא אֶל־הַצֹּאן וְקַח־לִי מִשָּׁם שְׁנֵי גְּדָיֵי עִזִּים טֹבִים וְאֶעֱשֶׂה אֹתָם מַטְעַמִּים לְאָבִיךָ כַּאֲשֶׁר אָהֵב (בראשית כז, ט)
ל־ד: לַמְנַצֵּחַ אֶל־הַנְּחִילוֹת מִזְמוֹר לְדָוִד (תהלים ה, א)
ל־ה: לַיהוָה הַיְשׁוּעָה עַל־עַמְּךָ בִרְכָתֶךָ סֶּלָה (תהלים ג, ט)
ל־ו: לָבְשׁוּ כָרִים הַצֹּאן וַעֲמָקִים יַעַטְפוּ־בָר יִתְרוֹעֲעוּ אַף יָשִׁירוּ (תהלים סה, יד)
ל־ז: לָרֹכֵב בִּשְׁמֵי שְׁמֵי־קֶדֶם הֵן יִתֵּן בְּקוֹלוֹ קוֹל עֹז (תהלים סח, לד)
ל־ח: לָכֵן שָׂמַח לִבִּי וַיָּגֶל כְּבוֹדִי אַף־בְּשָׂרִי יִשְׁכֹּן לָבֶטַח (תהלים טז, ט)
ל־ט: לֹא־יִכּוֹן אָדָם בְּרֶשַׁע וְשֹׁרֶשׁ צַדִּיקִים בַּל־יִמּוֹט (משלי יב, ג)
ל־י: לוּלֵי תוֹרָתְךָ שַׁעֲשֻׁעָי אָז אָבַדְתִּי בְעָנְיִי (תהלים קיט, צב)
ל־כ: לְמַעַן אֲסַפְּרָה כָּל־תְּהִלָּתֶיךָ בְּשַׁעֲרֵי בַת־צִיּוֹן אָגִילָה בִּישׁוּעָתֶךָ (תהלים ט, טו)
ל־ל: לֶאְסֹר מַלְכֵיהֶם בְּזִקִּים וְנִכְבְּדֵיהֶם בְּכַבְלֵי בַרְזֶל (תהלים קמט, ח)
ל־מ: לִקְדוֹשִׁים אֲשֶׁר־בָּאָרֶץ הֵמָּה וְאַדִּירֵי כָּל־חֶפְצִי־בָם (תהלים קמט, ח)
ל־נ: לְעֻמַּת הַמִּסְגֶּרֶת תִּהְיֶיןָ הַטַּבָּעוֹת לְבָתִּים לְבַדִּים לָשֵׂאת אֶת־הַשֻּׁלְחָן (שמות כה, כז)
ל־ס: לֹא תִשָּׂא שֵׁמַע שָׁוְא אַל־תָּשֶׁת יָדְךָ עִם־רָשָׁע לִהְיֹת עֵד חָמָס (שמות כג, א)
ל־ע: לֶחֶם אַבִּירִים אָכַל אִישׁ צֵידָה שָׁלַח לָהֶם לָשֹׂבַע (תהלים עח, כה)

זיו השמות

ל-פ: לַמְנַצֵּחַ עַל הַגִּתִּית לְאָסָף (תהלים פא, א)
ל-צ: לְכוּ חֲזוּ מִפְעֲלוֹת יְהֹוָה אֲשֶׁר שָׂם שַׁמּוֹת בָּאָרֶץ (תהלים מו, ט)
ל-ק: לְלֵוִי חֲשַׁבְיָה בֶּן קְמוּאֵל לְאַהֲרֹן צָדוֹק (דברי הימים-א כז, יז)
ל-ר: לְךָ דֻמִיָּה תְהִלָּה אֱלֹהִים בְּצִיּוֹן וּלְךָ יְשֻׁלַּם נֶדֶר (תהלים סה, ב)
ל-ש: לְךָ אָמַר לִבִּי בַּקְּשׁוּ פָנָי אֶת פָּנֶיךָ יְהֹוָה אֲבַקֵּשׁ (תהלים כז, ח)
ל-ת: לַמְנַצֵּחַ עַל שֹׁשַׁנִּים לִבְנֵי קֹרַח מַשְׂכִּיל שִׁיר יְדִידֹת (תהלים מה, א)

מ

מ-א: מוֹנֶה מִסְפָּר לַכּוֹכָבִים לְכֻלָּם שֵׁמוֹת יִקְרָא (תהלים קמז, ד)
מ-ב: מָגִנִּי עַל אֱלֹהִים מוֹשִׁיעַ יִשְׁרֵי לֵב (תהלים ז, יא)
מ-ד: מִזְמוֹר שִׁיר חֲנֻכַּת הַבַּיִת לְדָוִד (תהלים ל, א)
מ-ה: מַחֲשָׁבוֹת בְּעֵצָה תִכּוֹן וּבְתַחְבֻּלוֹת עֲשֵׂה מִלְחָמָה (משלי כ, יח)
מ-ו: מַה דּוֹדֵךְ מִדּוֹד הַיָּפָה בַּנָּשִׁים מַה דּוֹדֵךְ מִדּוֹד שֶׁכָּכָה הִשְׁבַּעְתָּנוּ (שיר השירים ה, ט)
מ-ז: מִזְמוֹר לְדָוִד הָבוּ לַיהֹוָה בְּנֵי אֵלִים הָבוּ לַיהֹוָה כָּבוֹד וָעֹז (תהלים כט, א)
מ-ח: מִן הָאָרֶץ הַהִוא יָצָא אַשּׁוּר וַיִּבֶן אֶת נִינְוֵה וְאֶת רְחֹבֹת עִיר וְאֶת כָּלַח (בראשית י, יא)
מ-ט: מִזְמוֹר לְאָסָף אֱלֹהִים נִצָּב בַּעֲדַת אֵל בְּקֶרֶב אֱלֹהִים יִשְׁפֹּט (תהלים פב, א)
מ-י: מָה אָהַבְתִּי תוֹרָתֶךָ כָּל הַיּוֹם הִיא שִׂיחָתִי (תהלים קיט, צז)
מ-כ: מִזְמוֹר לְדָוִד יְהֹוָה מִי יָגוּר בְּאָהֳלֶךָ מִי יִשְׁכֹּן בְּהַר קָדְשֶׁךָ (תהלים טו, א)
מ-ל: מַה טֹּבוּ אֹהָלֶיךָ יַעֲקֹב מִשְׁכְּנֹתֶיךָ יִשְׂרָאֵל (במדבר כד, ה)
מ-מ: מְאוֹר עֵינַיִם יְשַׂמַּח לֵב שְׁמוּעָה טוֹבָה תְּדַשֶּׁן עָצֶם (משלי טו, ל)
מ-נ: מַה יָּקָר חַסְדְּךָ אֱלֹהִים וּבְנֵי אָדָם בְּצֵל כְּנָפֶיךָ יֶחֱסָיוּן (תהלים לו, ח)
מ-ס: מְקוֹר חַיִּים פִּי צַדִּיק וּפִי רְשָׁעִים יְכַסֶּה חָמָס (משלי י, יא)
מ-ע: מִצִּיּוֹן מִכְלַל יֹפִי אֱלֹהִים הוֹפִיעַ (תהלים נ, ב)
מ-פ: מַרְכְּבֹת פַּרְעֹה וְחֵילוֹ יָרָה בַיָּם וּמִבְחַר שָׁלִשָׁיו טֻבְּעוּ בְיַם סוּף (שמות טו, ד)
מ-צ: מִמְּכוֹן שִׁבְתּוֹ הִשְׁגִּיחַ אֶל כָּל יֹשְׁבֵי הָאָרֶץ (תהלים לג, יד)
מ-ק: מַיִם קָרִים עַל נֶפֶשׁ עֲיֵפָה וּשְׁמוּעָה טוֹבָה מֵאֶרֶץ מֶרְחָק (משלי כה, כה)
מ-ר: מִי זֶה הָאִישׁ יְרֵא יְהֹוָה יוֹרֶנּוּ בְּדֶרֶךְ יִבְחָר (תהלים כה, יב)
מ-ש: מִנֹּגַהּ נֶגְדּוֹ עָבָיו עָבְרוּ בָּרָד וְגַחֲלֵי אֵשׁ (תהלים יח, יג)
מ-ת: מַה יְּדִידוֹת מִשְׁכְּנוֹתֶיךָ יְהֹוָה צְבָאוֹת (תהלים פד, ב)

נ

נ-א: נַפְשֵׁנוּ חִכְּתָה לַיהֹוָה עֶזְרֵנוּ וּמָגִנֵּנוּ הוּא (תהלים לג, כ)
נ-ב: נָטִיתִי לִבִּי לַעֲשׂוֹת חֻקֶּיךָ לְעוֹלָם עֵקֶב (תהלים קיט, קיב)
נ-ד: נִשְׁכַּחְתִּי כְּמֵת מִלֵּב הָיִיתִי כִּכְלִי אֹבֵד (תהלים לא, יג)
נ-ה: נְקִי כַפַּיִם וּבַר לֵבָב אֲשֶׁר לֹא נָשָׂא לַשָּׁוְא נַפְשִׁי וְלֹא נִשְׁבַּע לְמִרְמָה (תהלים כד, ד)
נ-ו: נָתַתָּה שִׂמְחָה בְלִבִּי מֵעֵת דְּגָנָם וְתִירוֹשָׁם רָבּוּ (תהלים ד, ח)

What's in a Name

נ-ז: נַחַל קִישׁוֹן גְּרָפָם נַחַל קְדוּמִים נַחַל קִישׁוֹן תִּדְרְכִי נַפְשִׁי עֹז (שופטים ה, כא)

נ-ח: נֶגְבָּה לְאֶפְרַיִם וְצָפוֹנָה לִמְנַשֶּׁה וַיְהִי הַיָּם גְּבוּלוֹ וּבְאָשֵׁר יִפְגְּעוּן מִצָּפוֹן וּבְיִשָּׂשכָר מִמִּזְרָח (יהושע יז, י)

נ-י: נָכוֹן לִבִּי אֱלֹהִים אָשִׁירָה וַאֲזַמְּרָה אַף כְּבוֹדִי (תהלים קח, ב)

נ-כ: נְרַנְּנָה בִּישׁוּעָתֶךָ וּבְשֵׁם אֱלֹהֵינוּ נִדְגֹּל יְמַלֵּא יְהוָה כָּל מִשְׁאֲלוֹתֶיךָ (תהלים כ, ו)

נ-ל: נֶחְשַׁבְתִּי עִם יוֹרְדֵי בוֹר הָיִיתִי כְּגֶבֶר אֵין אֱיָל (תהלים פח, ה)

נ-מ: נַעַר הָיִיתִי גַּם זָקַנְתִּי וְלֹא רָאִיתִי צַדִּיק נֶעֱזָב וְזַרְעוֹ מְבַקֶּשׁ לָחֶם (תהלים לז, כה)

נ-נ: נָהָר פְּלָגָיו יְשַׂמְּחוּ עִיר אֱלֹהִים קְדֹשׁ מִשְׁכְּנֵי עֶלְיוֹן (תהלים מו, ה)

נ-ס: נַפְתָּלִי לֹא הוֹרִישׁ אֶת יֹשְׁבֵי בֵית שֶׁמֶשׁ וְאֶת יֹשְׁבֵי בֵית עֲנָת וַיֵּשֶׁב בְּקֶרֶב הַכְּנַעֲנִי יֹשְׁבֵי הָאָרֶץ וְיֹשְׁבֵי בֵית שֶׁמֶשׁ וּבֵית עֲנָת הָיוּ לָהֶם לָמַס (שופטים א, לג)

נ-פ: נִפְלָאוֹת בְּאֶרֶץ חָם נוֹרָאוֹת עַל יַם סוּף (תהלים קו, כב)

נ-צ: נַפְשׁוֹ בְּטוֹב תָּלִין וְזַרְעוֹ יִירַשׁ אָרֶץ (תהלים כה, יג)

נ-ק: נִשְׁבַּע יְהוָה וְלֹא יִנָּחֵם אַתָּה כֹהֵן לְעוֹלָם עַל דִּבְרָתִי מַלְכִּי צֶדֶק (תהלים קי, ד)

נ-ר: נַפְשִׁי לַאדֹנָי מִשֹּׁמְרִים לַבֹּקֶר שֹׁמְרִים לַבֹּקֶר (תהלים קל, ו)

נ-ש: נָשַׁמּוּ מְסִלּוֹת שָׁבַת עֹבֵר אֹרַח הֵפֵר בְּרִית מָאַס עָרִים לֹא חָשַׁב אֱנוֹשׁ (ישעיה לג, ח)

נ-ת: נִמְצְאוּ דְבָרֶיךָ וָאֹכְלֵם וַיְהִי דְבָרְךָ לִי לְשָׂשׂוֹן וּלְשִׂמְחַת לְבָבִי כִּי נִקְרָא שִׁמְךָ עָלַי יְהוָה אֱלֹהֵי צְבָאוֹת (ירמיה טו, טז)

ס

ס-ד: סְעָדֵנִי וְאִוָּשֵׁעָה וְאֶשְׁעָה בְחֻקֶּיךָ תָמִיד (תהלים קיט, קיז)

ס-ה: סֹבּוּ צִיּוֹן וְהַקִּיפוּהָ סִפְרוּ מִגְדָּלֶיהָ (תהלים מח, יג)

ס-ו: סוּר מֵרָע וַעֲשֵׂה טוֹב בַּקֵּשׁ שָׁלוֹם וְרָדְפֵהוּ (תהלים לד, טו)

ס-י: סֵעֲפִים שָׂנֵאתִי וְתוֹרָתְךָ אָהָבְתִּי (תהלים קיט, קיג)

ס-כ: סְגָנִים הִשְׁבַּתָּ כָּל רִשְׁעֵי אָרֶץ לָכֵן אֲהַבְתִּי עֵדֹתֶיךָ (תהלים קיט, קיט)

ס-ל: סוּרוּ מִנֵּי דֶרֶךְ הַטּוּ מִנֵּי אֹרַח הַשְׁבִּיתוּ מִפָּנֵינוּ אֶת קְדוֹשׁ יִשְׂרָאֵל (ישעיה ל, יא)

ס-מ: סוֹד יְהוָה לִירֵאָיו וּבְרִיתוֹ לְהוֹדִיעָם (תהלים כה, יד)

ס-נ: סִיחוֹן מֶלֶךְ הָאֱמֹרִי הַיּוֹשֵׁב בְּחֶשְׁבּוֹן מֹשֵׁל מֵעֲרוֹעֵר אֲשֶׁר עַל שְׂפַת נַחַל אַרְנוֹן וְתוֹךְ הַנַּחַל וַחֲצִי הַגִּלְעָד וְעַד יַבֹּק הַנַּחַל גְּבוּל בְּנֵי עַמּוֹן (יהושע יב, ב)

ס-ע: סָלוּ עָמוֹק חִלְקִיָּה יְדַעְיָה אֵלֶּה רָאשֵׁי הַכֹּהֲנִים וַאֲחֵיהֶם בִּימֵי יֵשׁוּעַ (נחמיה יב, ז)

ס-צ: סָפְקוּ עָלַיִךְ כַּפַּיִם כָּל עֹבְרֵי דֶרֶךְ שָׁרְקוּ וַיָּנִעוּ רֹאשָׁם עַל בַּת יְרוּשָׁלִָם הֲזֹאת הָעִיר שֶׁיֹּאמְרוּ כְּלִילַת יֹפִי מָשׂוֹשׂ לְכָל הָאָרֶץ (איכה ב, טו)

ס-ר: סְמוּכִים לָעַד לְעוֹלָם עֲשׂוּיִם בֶּאֱמֶת וְיָשָׁר (תהלים קיא, ח)

ס-ת: סַכֹּתָה בָאַף וַתִּרְדְּפֵנוּ הָרַגְתָּ לֹא חָמָלְתָּ (איכה ג, מג)

ע

ע-א: עַתָּה אָקוּם יֹאמַר יְהוָה עַתָּה אֵרוֹמָם עַתָּה אֶנָּשֵׂא (ישעיה לג, י)

ע-ב: עַד אֶמְצָא מָקוֹם לַיהוָה מִשְׁכָּנוֹת לַאֲבִיר יַעֲקֹב (תהלים קלב, ה)

ע-ד: עָלֶיךָ נִסְמַכְתִּי מִבֶּטֶן מִמְּעֵי אִמִּי אַתָּה גוֹזִי בְּךָ תְהִלָּתִי תָמִיד (תהלים עא, ו)
ע-ה: עָזִּי וְזִמְרָת יָהּ וַיְהִי-לִי לִישׁוּעָה (תהלים קיח יד)
ע-ו: עַתָּה יָדַעְתִּי כִּי הוֹשִׁיעַ יְהוָה מְשִׁיחוֹ יַעֲנֵהוּ מִשְּׁמֵי קָדְשׁוֹ בִּגְבֻרוֹת יֵשַׁע יְמִינוֹ (תהלים כ, ז)
ע-ז: עַל כֵּן אָהַבְתִּי מִצְוֹתֶיךָ מִזָּהָב וּמִפָּז (תהלים קיט, קכז)
ע-ח: עוּרָה לָמָּה תִישַׁן אֲדֹנָי הָקִיצָה אַל תִּזְנַח לָנֶצַח (תהלים מד, כד)
ע-ט: עֹשֶׂה מַלְאָכָיו רוּחוֹת מְשָׁרְתָיו אֵשׁ לֹהֵט (תהלים קד, ד)
ע-י: עֶרֶב וָבֹקֶר וְצָהֳרַיִם אָשִׂיחָה וְאֶהֱמֶה וַיִּשְׁמַע קוֹלִי (תהלים נה, יח)
ע-כ: עָלַי אֱלֹהִים נְדָרֶיךָ אֲשַׁלֵּם תּוֹדֹת לָךְ (תהלים נו, יג)
ע-ל: עַל דַּעְתְּךָ כִּי לֹא אֶרְשָׁע וְאֵין מִיָּדְךָ מַצִּיל (איוב י, ז)
ע-מ: עִם חָסִיד תִּתְחַסָּד עִם גְּבַר תָּמִים תִּתַּמָּם (תהלים יח, כו)
ע-נ: עֲטֶרֶת שְׁנַת טוֹבָתֶךָ וּמַעְגָּלֶיךָ יִרְעֲפוּן דָּשֶׁן (תהלים סה, יב)
ע-ס: עַל כֵּן כָּל יָדַיִם תִּרְפֶּינָה וְכָל לְבַב אֱנוֹשׁ יִמָּס (ישעיה יג, ז)
ע-ע: עֵדוּת בִּיהוֹסֵף שָׂמוֹ בְּצֵאתוֹ עַל אֶרֶץ מִצְרָיִם שְׂפַת לֹא יָדַעְתִּי אֶשְׁמָע (תהלים פא, ו)
ע-פ: עַמּוּדֵיהֶם עֶשְׂרִים וְאַדְנֵיהֶם עֶשְׂרִים נְחֹשֶׁת וָוֵי הָעַמּוּדִים וַחֲשֻׁקֵיהֶם כָּסֶף (שמות לח, י)
ע-צ: עֶזְרִי מֵעִם יְהוָה עֹשֵׂה שָׁמַיִם וָאָרֶץ (תהלים קכא, ב)
ע-ק: עַם גָּדוֹל וָרָם בְּנֵי עֲנָקִים אֲשֶׁר אַתָּה יָדַעְתָּ וְאַתָּה שָׁמַעְתָּ מִי יִתְיַצֵּב לִפְנֵי בְּנֵי עֲנָק (דברים ט, ב)
ע-ר: עֹשֶׂה גְדֹלוֹת וְאֵין חֵקֶר נִפְלָאוֹת עַד אֵין מִסְפָּר (איוב ה, ט)
ע-ש: עַל מֶה נִאֵץ רָשָׁע אֱלֹהִים אָמַר בְּלִבּוֹ לֹא תִדְרֹשׁ (תהלים י, יג)
ע-ת: עֲשֵׂה לְךָ שְׁתֵּי חֲצוֹצְרֹת כֶּסֶף מִקְשָׁה תַּעֲשֶׂה אֹתָם וְהָיוּ לְךָ לְמִקְרָא הָעֵדָה וּלְמַסַּע אֶת הַמַּחֲנוֹת (במדבר י, ב)

פ

פ-א: פָּתוֹת אֹתָהּ פִּתִּים וְיָצַקְתָּ עָלֶיהָ שָׁמֶן מִנְחָה הִוא (ויקרא ב, ו)
פ-ב: פַּעֲמֹן זָהָב וְרִמּוֹן פַּעֲמֹן זָהָב וְרִמּוֹן עַל-שׁוּלֵי הַמְּעִיל סָבִיב (שמות כח, לד)
פ-ג: פָּצוּ עָלַי פִּיהֶם אַרְיֵה טֹרֵף וְשֹׁאֵג (תהלים כב, יד)
פ-ד: פִּזַּר נָתַן לָאֶבְיוֹנִים צִדְקָתוֹ עֹמֶדֶת לָעַד קַרְנוֹ תָּרוּם בְּכָבוֹד (תהלים קיב, ט)
פ-ה: פָּרַשׂ עָנָן לְמָסָךְ וְאֵשׁ לְהָאִיר לָיְלָה (תהלים קה, לט)
פ-ה: פִּתְחוּ לִי שַׁעֲרֵי צֶדֶק אָבֹא בָם אוֹדֶה יָהּ (תהלים קיח, יט)
פ-ו: פְּדוּת שָׁלַח לְעַמּוֹ צִוָּה לְעוֹלָם בְּרִיתוֹ קָדוֹשׁ וְנוֹרָא שְׁמוֹ (תהלים קיא, ט)
פ-ט: פִּי-צַדִּיק יֶהְגֶּה חָכְמָה וּלְשׁוֹנוֹ תְּדַבֵּר מִשְׁפָּט (תהלים לז, ל)
פ-י: פָּדָה בְשָׁלוֹם נַפְשִׁי מִקֲּרָב לִי כִּי בְרַבִּים הָיוּ עִמָּדִי (תהלים נה, יט)
פ-כ: פָּנֶיךָ הָאֵר בְּעַבְדֶּךָ וְלַמְּדֵנִי אֶת חֻקֶּיךָ (תהלים קיט, קלה)
פ-ל: פֶּן יִטְרֹף כְּאַרְיֵה נַפְשִׁי פֹּרֵק וְאֵין מַצִּיל (תהלים ז, ג)
פ-מ: פִּקּוּדֵי יְהוָה יְשָׁרִים מְשַׂמְּחֵי לֵב מִצְוַת יְהוָה בָּרָה מְאִירַת עֵינָיִם (תהלים יט, ט)
פ-נ: פּוֹתֵחַ אֶת יָדֶךָ וּמַשְׂבִּיעַ לְכָל חַי רָצוֹן (תהלים קמה, טז)

פ-ס: פֶּלֶס וּמֹאזְנֵי מִשְׁפָּט לַיהֹוָה מַעֲשֵׂהוּ כָּל אַבְנֵי כִיס (משלי טז, יא)

פ-ע: פַּאֲרֵי פִשְׁתִּים יִהְיוּ עַל רֹאשָׁם וּמִכְנְסֵי פִשְׁתִּים יִהְיוּ עַל מָתְנֵיהֶם לֹא יַחְגְּרוּ בַּיָּזַע (יחזקאל מד, יח)

פ-פ: פָּתַח פִּיךָ לְאִלֵּם אֶל דִּין כָּל בְּנֵי חֲלוֹף (משלי לא, ח)

פ-צ: פָּנִיתָ לְפָנֶיהָ וַתַּשְׁרֵשׁ שָׁרָשֶׁיהָ וַתְּמַלֵּא אָרֶץ (תהלים פ, י)

פ-ר: פָּתַח צוּר וַיָּזוּבוּ מָיִם הָלְכוּ בַּצִּיּוֹת נָהָר (תהלים קה, מא)

פ-ש: פָּנִים בְּפָנִים דִּבֶּר יְהֹוָה עִמָּכֶם בָּהָר מִתּוֹךְ הָאֵשׁ (דברים ה, ד)

פ-ת: פִּי יְדַבֵּר חָכְמוֹת וְהָגוּת לִבִּי תְבוּנוֹת (תהלים מט, ד)

צ

צ-א: צִפְנָיָה צָפַן-רוּחַ וְשֶׁמֶן יְמִינוֹ יִקְרָא (משלי כז, טז)

צ-ב: צִדְקָתְךָ לֹא-כִסִּיתִי בְּתוֹךְ לִבִּי אֱמוּנָתְךָ וּתְשׁוּעָתְךָ אָמָרְתִּי לֹא-כִחַדְתִּי חַסְדְּךָ וַאֲמִתְּךָ לְקָהָל רָב (תהלים מ, יא)

צ-ד: צִוִּיתָ צֶדֶק עֵדֹתֶיךָ וֶאֱמוּנָה מְאֹד (תהלים קיט, קלח)

צ-ה: צַדִּיקִים יִירְשׁוּ-אָרֶץ וְיִשְׁכְּנוּ לָעַד עָלֶיהָ (תהלים לז, כט)

צ-ה: צִיּוֹן בְּמִשְׁפָּט תִּפָּדֶה וְשָׁבֶיהָ בִּצְדָקָה (ישעיה א, פז)

צ-ו: צַוֵּה אֱלֹהֶיךָ עֻזֶּךָ עוּזָּה אֱלֹהִים זוּ פָּעַלְתָּ לָּנוּ (תהלים סח, כט)

צ-ח: צִיּוֹן יִשְׁאָלוּ דֶּרֶךְ הֵנָּה פְנֵיהֶם בֹּאוּ וְנִלְווּ אֶל יְהֹוָה בְּרִית עוֹלָם לֹא תִשָּׁכֵחַ (ירמיה נ, ה)

צ-י: צַר וּמָצוֹק מְצָאוּנִי מִצְוֹתֶיךָ שַׁעֲשֻׁעָי (תהלים קיט, קמג)

צ-כ: צֶדֶק וּמִשְׁפָּט מְכוֹן כִּסְאֶךָ חֶסֶד וֶאֱמֶת יְקַדְּמוּ פָנֶיךָ (תהלים פט, טו)

צ-ל: צַהֲלִי וָרֹנִּי יוֹשֶׁבֶת צִיּוֹן כִּי גָדוֹל בְּקִרְבֵּךְ קְדוֹשׁ יִשְׂרָאֵל (ישעיה יב, ו)

צ-מ: צִפּוֹר שָׁמַיִם וּדְגֵי הַיָּם עֹבֵר אָרְחוֹת יַמִּים (תהלים ח, ט)

צ-נ: צַוֵּה אֶת הַכֹּהֲנִים נֹשְׂאֵי אֲרוֹן הָעֵדוּת וְיַעֲלוּ מִן הַיַּרְדֵּן (יהושע ד, טז)

צ-ע: צִדְקַת תָּמִים תְּיַשֵּׁר דַּרְכּוֹ וּבְרִשְׁעָתוֹ יִפֹּל רָשָׁע (משלי יא, ה)

צ-צ: צַדִּיק לְעוֹלָם בַּל יִמּוֹט וּרְשָׁעִים לֹא יִשְׁכְּנוּ אָרֶץ (משלי י, ל)

צ-ק: צַוָּארֵךְ כְּמִגְדַּל הַשֵּׁן עֵינַיִךְ בְּרֵכוֹת בְּחֶשְׁבּוֹן עַל שַׁעַר בַּת רַבִּים אַפֵּךְ כְּמִגְדַּל הַלְּבָנוֹן צוֹפֶה פְּנֵי דַמָּשֶׂק (שה״ש ז, ה)

צ-ר: צִידֹנִים יִקְרְאוּ לְחֶרְמוֹן שִׂרְיֹן וְהָאֱמֹרִי יִקְרְאוּ לוֹ שְׂנִיר (דברים ג, ט)

צ-ש: צַו אֶת בְּנֵי יִשְׂרָאֵל וִישַׁלְּחוּ מִן הַמַּחֲנֶה כָּל צָרוּעַ וְכָל-זָב וְכֹל טָמֵא לָנָפֶשׁ (במדבר ה, ב)

צ-ת: צִדְקָתְךָ צֶדֶק לְעוֹלָם וְתוֹרָתְךָ אֱמֶת (תהלים קיט, קמב)

ק

ק-א: קַדֶּשׁ לִי כָל בְּכוֹר פֶּטֶר כָּל רֶחֶם בִּבְנֵי יִשְׂרָאֵל בָּאָדָם וּבַבְּהֵמָה לִי הוּא (שמות יג, ב)

ק-ב: קָרְבוּ רִיבְכֶם יֹאמַר יְהֹוָה הַגִּישׁוּ עֲצֻמוֹתֵיכֶם יֹאמַר מֶלֶךְ יַעֲקֹב (ישעיה מא, כא)

ק-ד: קוֹל יְהֹוָה יְחוֹלֵל אַיָּלוֹת וַיֶּחֱשֹׂף יְעָרוֹת וּבְהֵיכָלוֹ כֻּלּוֹ אֹמֵר כָּבוֹד (תהלים כט, ט)

ק-ה: קוֹלִי אֶל יְהֹוָה אֶקְרָא וַיַּעֲנֵנִי מֵהַר קָדְשׁוֹ סֶלָה (תהלים ג, ה)

זיו השמות

ק-ו: קוּמִי שְׂאִי אֶת הַנַּעַר וְהַחֲזִיקִי אֶת יָדֵךְ בּוֹ כִּי לְגוֹי גָּדוֹל אֲשִׂימֶנּוּ (בראשית כא, יח)
ק-ח: קַח נָא אֶת בִּרְכָתִי אֲשֶׁר הֻבָאת לָךְ כִּי חַנַּנִי אֱלֹהִים וְכִי יֶשׁ לִי כֹל וַיִּפְצַר בּוֹ וַיִּקָּח (בראשית כא, יח)
ק-ט: קְחוּ לָכֶם מִן הָעָם שְׁנֵים עָשָׂר אֲנָשִׁים אִישׁ אֶחָד אִישׁ אֶחָד מִשָּׁבֶט (יהושע ד, ב)
ק-י: קִוִּיתִי יְהֹוָה קִוְּתָה נַפְשִׁי וְלִדְבָרוֹ הוֹחָלְתִּי (תהלים קל, ה)
ק-כ: קוּמָה עֶזְרָתָה לָּנוּ וּפְדֵנוּ לְמַעַן חַסְדֶּךָ (תהלים מד, כז)
ק-ל: קוֹל רִנָּה וִישׁוּעָה בְּאָהֳלֵי צַדִּיקִים יְמִין יְהוָה עֹשָׂה חָיִל (תהלים קיח, טו)
ק-מ: קַח אֶת הַלְוִיִּם מִתּוֹךְ בְּנֵי יִשְׂרָאֵל וְטִהַרְתָּ אֹתָם (במדבר ח, ו)
ק-נ: קוֹלִי אֶל יְהוָה אֶזְעָק קוֹלִי אֶל יְהוָה אֶתְחַנָּן (תהלים קמ, ב)
ק-ע: קָרוֹב יְהוָה לְנִשְׁבְּרֵי לֵב וְאֶת דַּכְּאֵי רוּחַ יוֹשִׁיעַ (תהלים לד, יט)
ק-פ: קְנֹה חָכְמָה מַה טּוֹב מֵחָרוּץ וּקְנוֹת בִּינָה נִבְחָר מִכָּסֶף (משלי טז)
ק-צ: קוֹל רַעַמְךָ בַּגַּלְגַּל הֵאִירוּ בְרָקִים תֵּבֵל רָגְזָה וַתִּרְעַשׁ הָאָרֶץ (תהלים עז, יט)
ק-ר: קוֹל יְהוָה בַּכֹּחַ קוֹל יְהוָה בֶּהָדָר (תהלים כט, ד)
ק-ש: קוֹל יְהוָה חֹצֵב לַהֲבוֹת אֵשׁ (תהלים כט, ז)
ק-ת: קָרוֹב אַתָּה יְהוָה וְכָל מִצְוֹתֶיךָ אֱמֶת (תהלים קיט, קנא)

ר

ר-א: רוֹמְמוּ יְהוָה אֱלֹהֵינוּ וְהִשְׁתַּחֲווּ לַהֲדֹם רַגְלָיו קָדוֹשׁ הוּא (תהלים צט, ה)
ר-ב: רָצִיתָ יְהוָה אַרְצֶךָ שַׁבְתָּ שְׁבִית יַעֲקֹב (תהלים פה, ב)
ר-ד: רַחוּם וְחַנּוּן יְהוָה אֶרֶךְ אַפַּיִם וְרַב חָסֶד (תהלים קג, ח)
ר-ה: רַבּוֹת רָעוֹת צַדִּיק וּמִכֻּלָּם יַצִּילֶנּוּ יְהוָה (תהלים לד, כ)
ר-ה: רִגְזוּ וְאַל תֶּחֱטָאוּ אִמְרוּ בִלְבַבְכֶם עַל מִשְׁכַּבְכֶם וְדֹמּוּ סֶלָה (תהלים ד, ה)
ר-ו: רוֹמְמוּ יְהוָה אֱלֹהֵינוּ וְהִשְׁתַּחֲווּ לְהַר קָדְשׁוֹ כִּי קָדוֹשׁ יְהוָה אֱלֹהֵינוּ (תהלים צט, ט)
ר-ז: רְאוּבֵן בְּכֹרִי אַתָּה כֹּחִי וְרֵאשִׁית אוֹנִי יֶתֶר שְׂאֵת וְיֶתֶר עָז (בראשית מט, ג)
ר-ח: רוּחַ אֲדֹנָי יֱהֹוִה עָלָי יַעַן מָשַׁח יהוה אֹתִי לְבַשֵּׂר עֲנָוִים שְׁלָחַנִי לַחֲבֹשׁ לְנִשְׁבְּרֵי לֵב לִקְרֹא לִשְׁבוּיִם דְּרוֹר וְלַאֲסוּרִים פְּקַח קוֹחַ (ישעיה סא, א)
ר-ט: רָאִיתִי אֶת אֲדֹנָי נִצָּב עַל הַמִּזְבֵּחַ וַיֹּאמֶר הַךְ הַכַּפְתּוֹר וְיִרְעֲשׁוּ הַסִּפִּים וּבְצַעַם בְּרֹאשׁ כֻּלָּם וְאַחֲרִיתָם בַּחֶרֶב אֶהֱרֹג לֹא יָנוּס לָהֶם נָס וְלֹא יִמָּלֵט לָהֶם פָּלִיט (עמוס ט, א)
ר-י: רְאֵה כִּי פִקּוּדֶיךָ אָהָבְתִּי יְהוָה כְּחַסְדְּךָ חַיֵּנִי (תהלים קיט, קנט)
ר-כ: רוּמָה יְהוָה בְעֻזֶּךָ נָשִׁירָה וּנְזַמְּרָה גְּבוּרָתֶךָ (תהלים כא, יד)
ר-ל: רְאוּ עַתָּה כִּי אֲנִי אֲנִי הוּא וְאֵין אֱלֹהִים עִמָּדִי אֲנִי אָמִית וַאֲחַיֶּה מָחַצְתִּי וַאֲנִי אֶרְפָּא וְאֵין מִיָּדִי מַצִּיל (דברים לב, לט)
ר-מ: רָאוּ עֲנָוִים יִשְׂמָחוּ דֹּרְשֵׁי אֱלֹהִים וִיחִי לְבַבְכֶם (תהלים סט, לג)
ר-נ: רְאֵה זֶה מָצָאתִי אָמְרָה קֹהֶלֶת אַחַת לְאַחַת לִמְצֹא חֶשְׁבּוֹן (קהלת ז, כז)
ר-ע: רְאֵה נָתַתִּי לְפָנֶיךָ הַיּוֹם אֶת הַחַיִּים וְאֶת הַטּוֹב וְאֶת הַמָּוֶת וְאֶת הָרָע (דברים ל, טו)
ר-פ: רְעֵבִים גַּם צְמֵאִים נַפְשָׁם בָּהֶם תִּתְעַטָּף (תהלים קז, ה)

ר-צ: רָעָה הִתְרֹעֲעָה הָאָרֶץ פּוֹר הִתְפּוֹרְרָה אֶרֶץ מוֹט הִתְמוֹטְטָה אָרֶץ (ישעיה כד, יט)
ר-ק: רֵעֲךָ וְרֵעַ אָבִיךָ אַל תַּעֲזֹב וּבֵית אָחִיךָ אַל תָּבוֹא בְּיוֹם אֵידֶךָ טוֹב שָׁכֵן קָרוֹב מֵאָח רָחוֹק (משלי כז, י)
ר-ר: רָחַשׁ לִבִּי דָּבָר טוֹב אֹמֵר אָנִי מַעֲשַׂי לְמֶלֶךְ לְשׁוֹנִי עֵט סוֹפֵר מָהִיר (תהלים מה, ב)
ר-ש: רָאוּ הֲלִיכוֹתֶיךָ אֱלֹהִים הֲלִיכוֹת אֵלִי מַלְכִּי בַקֹּדֶשׁ (תהלים סח, כה)
ר-ת: רָאוּךָ מַּיִם אֱלֹהִים רָאוּךָ מַּיִם יָחִילוּ אַף יִרְגְּזוּ תְהֹמוֹת (תהלים עז, יז)

ש

ש-א: שַׂמֵּחַ נֶפֶשׁ עַבְדֶּךָ כִּי אֵלֶיךָ אֲדֹנָי נַפְשִׁי אֶשָּׂא (תהלים פו, ד)
ש-ב: שׁוּבָה יְהוָה אֶת-שְׁבִיתֵנוּ כַּאֲפִיקִים בַּנֶּגֶב (תהלים קכו, ד)
ש-ג: שָׁקַדְתִּי וָאֶהְיֶה כְּצִפּוֹר בּוֹדֵד עַל-גָּג (תהלים קב, ח)
ש-ד: שְׂאוּ שְׁעָרִים רָאשֵׁיכֶם וְהִנָּשְׂאוּ פִּתְחֵי עוֹלָם וְיָבוֹא מֶלֶךְ הַכָּבוֹד (תהלים כד, ז)
ש-ה: שִׁיר הַשִּׁירִים אֲשֶׁר לִשְׁלֹמֹה (שיר-השירים א, א)
ש-ה: שְׂאוּ יְדֵיכֶם קֹדֶשׁ וּבָרְכוּ אֶת יְהוָה (תהלים קלד, ב)
ש-ו: שְׁמַע תְּפִלָּה עָדֶיךָ כָּל-בָּשָׂר יָבֹאוּ (תהלים סה, ג)
ש-ח: שָׁמַע יְהוָה תְּחִנָּתִי יְהוָה תְּפִלָּתִי יִקָּח (תהלים ו, י)
ש-ט: שִׁוִּיתִי יְהוָה לְנֶגְדִּי תָמִיד כִּי מִימִינִי בַּל-אֶמּוֹט (תהלים טז, ח)
ש-י: שָׂנֵאתִי הַשֹּׁמְרִים הַבְלֵי-שָׁוְא וַאֲנִי אֶל-יְהוָה בָּטָחְתִּי (תהלים לא, ז)
ש-כ: שְׁלַח אוֹרְךָ וַאֲמִתְּךָ הֵמָּה יַנְחוּנִי יְבִיאוּנִי אֶל הַר קָדְשְׁךָ וְאֶל מִשְׁכְּנוֹתֶיךָ (תהלים מג, ג)
ש-ל: שָׁלוֹם רָב לְאֹהֲבֵי תוֹרָתֶךָ וְאֵין לָמוֹ מִכְשׁוֹל (תהלים קיט, קסה)
ש-מ: שְׁמָר תָּם וּרְאֵה יָשָׁר כִּי אַחֲרִית לְאִישׁ שָׁלוֹם (תהלים לז, לז)
ש-נ: שִׁיתוּ לִבְּכֶם לְחֵילָה פַּסְּגוּ אַרְמְנוֹתֶיהָ לְמַעַן תְּסַפְּרוּ לְדוֹר אַחֲרוֹן (תהלים מח, יד)
ש-ע: שִׂימָה נָּא עָרְבֵנִי עִמָּךְ מִי הוּא לְיָדִי יִתָּקֵעַ (איוב יז, ג)
ש-פ: שִׁיר מִזְמוֹר לְאָסָף (תהלים פג, א)
ש-צ: שִׁירוּ לַיהוָה שִׁיר חָדָשׁ שִׁירוּ לַיהוָה כָּל הָאָרֶץ (תהלים צו, א)
ש-ק: שֹׁפְטִים וְשֹׁטְרִים תִּתֶּן לְךָ בְּכָל שְׁעָרֶיךָ אֲשֶׁר יְהוָה אֱלֹהֶיךָ נֹתֵן לְךָ לִשְׁבָטֶיךָ וְשָׁפְטוּ אֶת הָעָם מִשְׁפַּט צֶדֶק (דברים טז, יח)
ש-ר: שְׂפַת אֱמֶת תִּכּוֹן לָעַד וְעַד אַרְגִּיעָה לְשׁוֹן שָׁקֶר (משלי יב, יט)
ש-ש: שִׁבְעַת יָמִים יִלְבָּשָׁם הַכֹּהֵן תַּחְתָּיו מִבָּנָיו אֲשֶׁר יָבֹא אֶל-אֹהֶל מוֹעֵד לְשָׁרֵת בַּקֹּדֶשׁ (שמות כט, ל)
ש-ת: שִׁיר הַמַּעֲלוֹת הִנֵּה בָּרְכוּ אֶת יְהוָה כָּל עַבְדֵי יְהוָה הָעֹמְדִים בְּבֵית יְהוָה בַּלֵּילוֹת (תהלים קלד, א)

ת

ת-א: תּוֹעֲבַת מְלָכִים עֲשׂוֹת רֶשַׁע כִּי בִצְדָקָה יִכּוֹן כִּסֵּא (משלי טז, יב)
ת-ב: תִּתֵּן לָהֶם יִלְקֹטוּן תִּפְתַּח יָדְךָ יִשְׂבְּעוּן טוֹב (תהלים קד, כח)
ת-ד: תְּהִלָּה לְדָוִד אֲרוֹמִמְךָ אֱלוֹהַי הַמֶּלֶךְ וַאֲבָרֲכָה שִׁמְךָ לְעוֹלָם וָעֶד (תהלים קמה, א)
ת-ה: תַּעֲרֹךְ לְפָנַי שֻׁלְחָן נֶגֶד צֹרְרָי דִּשַּׁנְתָּ בַשֶּׁמֶן רֹאשִׁי כּוֹסִי רְוָיָה (תהלים כג, ה)

ת-ו : תַּמְשִׁילֵהוּ בְּמַעֲשֵׂי יָדֶיךָ כֹּל שַׁתָּה תַחַת רַגְלָיו (תהלים ח, ז)

ת-ז : תֵּאָלַמְנָה שִׂפְתֵי שָׁקֶר הַדֹּבְרוֹת עַל צַדִּיק עָתָק בְּגַאֲוָה וָבוּז (תהלים לא, יט)

ת-ח : תּוֹדִיעֵנִי אֹרַח חַיִּים שֹׂבַע שְׂמָחוֹת אֶת פָּנֶיךָ נְעִמוֹת בִּימִינְךָ נֶצַח (תהלים טז, יא)

ת-ט : תַּחְתָּיו חַדּוּדֵי חָרֶשׂ יִרְפַּד חָרוּץ עֲלֵי טִיט (איוב מא, כב)

ת-י : תּוֹצִיאֵנִי מֵרֶשֶׁת זוּ טָמְנוּ לִי כִּי אַתָּה מָעוּזִי (תהלים לא, ה)

ת-כ : תַּאֲוַת עֲנָוִים שָׁמַעְתָּ יְהוָה תָּכִין לִבָּם תַּקְשִׁיב אָזְנֶךָ (תהלים י, יז)

ת-ל : תִּזְרֵם וְרוּחַ תִּשָּׂאֵם וּסְעָרָה תָּפִיץ אֹתָם וְאַתָּה תָּגִיל בַּיהוָה בִּקְדוֹשׁ יִשְׂרָאֵל תִּתְהַלָּל (ישעיה מא, טז)

ת-מ : תְּנוּ עֹז לֵאלֹהִים עַל יִשְׂרָאֵל גַּאֲוָתוֹ וְעֻזּוֹ בַּשְּׁחָקִים (תהלים סח, לה)

ת-נ : תְּחַטְּאֵנִי בְאֵזוֹב וְאֶטְהָר תְּכַבְּסֵנִי וּמִשֶּׁלֶג אַלְבִּין (תהלים נא, ט)

ת-ע : תַּאֲוָה נִהְיָה תֶּעֱרַב לְנָפֶשׁ וְתוֹעֲבַת כְּסִילִים סוּר מֵרָע (משלי יג, יט)

ת-פ : תִּקְרָא וְאָנֹכִי אֶעֱנֶךָּ לְמַעֲשֵׂה יָדֶיךָ תִכְסֹף (איוב יד, טו)

ת-צ : תַּחַת אֲבֹתֶיךָ יִהְיוּ בָנֶיךָ תְּשִׁיתֵמוֹ לְשָׂרִים בְּכָל-הָאָרֶץ (תהלים מה, יז)

ת-ק : תַּעַן לְשׁוֹנִי אִמְרָתֶךָ כִּי כָל מִצְוֹתֶיךָ צֶּדֶק (תהלים קיט, קעב)

ת-ר : תְּפִלָּה לְמֹשֶׁה אִישׁ הָאֱלֹהִים אֲדֹנָי מָעוֹן אַתָּה הָיִיתָ לָּנוּ בְּדֹר וָדֹר (תהלים צ, א)

ת-ש : תִּתְהַפֵּךְ כְּחֹמֶר חוֹתָם וְיִתְיַצְּבוּ כְּמוֹ לְבוּשׁ (איוב לח, יד)

ת-ת : תְּרַנֵּנָּה שְׂפָתַי כִּי אֲזַמְּרָה לָּךְ וְנַפְשִׁי אֲשֶׁר פָּדִיתָ (תהלים עא, כג)

לעילוי נשמת
הרה"ח הרה"ת ר' **רפאל משה הכהן** ז"ל
בן הרה"ח הרה"ת ר' יעקב מנחם מענדל הכהן ז"ל
שפּערלין

נפטר ליל ש"ק פ' לך לך
י"א מרחשון ה'תשנ"ו

ת.נ.צ.ב.ה.

לזכות כ״ק אדמו״ר מלך המשיח

ולזכות

החתן התמים **ארי׳ לייב הכהן** שיחי׳
בן הרה״ת ר׳ **רפאל משה הכהן** ע״ה

והכלה **מלכה צבי׳** שתחי׳

שפערלין

לרגלי נישואיהם בשעטומו״צ

אור לחי״י אלול

תהא שנת נפלאות **ח**רותינו

♦

נדפס ע״י הוריהם

מרת **דברא נעכא** שתחי׳ **שפערלין**

הרה״ת ר׳ ישעי׳ **אברהם** וזוג׳ מרת **רבקה** שיחיו
קמינקר

וזקניהם

מרת **חנה** שתחי׳ לייזער

מרת **דינה חנה** שתחי׳ קמינקר

הרה״ת ר׳ **צבי אבא** וזוג׳ מרת **מנוחה** שיחיו לרמן